JAN. 7 1992

35.73

33496

40 Years, 20 Million Ideas

The Toyota Suggestion System

40 Years,
20 Million Ideas

The Toyota Suggestion System

Yuzo Yasuda

Publisher's Message by
Norman Bodek
President, Productivity, Inc.

Productivity Press, Inc.

CAMBRIDGE, MASSACHUSETTS

NORWALK, CONNECTICUT

Originally published as *Toyota no sōi kufūteian katsudō,* copyright © 1989 by Japan Management Association, Tokyo. Translated into English by Productivity Press, Inc.

English edition copyright © 1991 by Productivity Press, Inc. Translated by Fredrich Czupryna.

All rights reserved. No part of this book may be reproduced or utilized in any form or by any means, electronic or mechanical, including photocopying, recording or by any information storage and retrieval system, without permission in writing from the publisher. Additional copies of this book are available from the publisher. Address all inquiries to:

Productivity Press, Inc.   Productivity, Inc.
P.O. Box 3007   or   101 Merritt 7 Corporate Park
Cambridge, MA 02140   Norwalk, CT 06856-5131
(617) 497-5146   (203) 846-3777

Cover design by Joyce Weston
Typeset by Rudra Press, Cambridge, MA
Printed and bound by Arcata Graphics Halliday
Printed in the United States of America

Library of Congress Cataloging-in-Publication Data
Yasuda, Yūdō
   Toyota no sōi kufū teian katsudō. English
   40 years, 20 million ideas: the creative idea suggestion system at Toyota/
   Yuzo Yasuda; foreword by Steve Ansuini; *translated by Fredrich Czupryna.*
p. cm.

   Translation of: Toyota no sōi kufū teian katsudō.
   Includes index.
ISBN 0-915299-74-7
1. Toyota Jidōsha Kabushiki Kaisha – Management.   2. Automobile industry
and trade – Japan – Management – Case studies.   3. Suggestion systems –
Japan – Case studies.   I. Title.   II. Title: Forty years, twenty million ideas.
HD 9710.J34T69313   1990   90-41841
338.7'6292'0952 – dc20
CIP

91 92 10 9 8 7 6 5 4 3 2 1

Contents

Publisher's Message

Something is wrong if workers do not look around each day, find things that are tedious or boring, and then rewrite the procedures. Even last month's manual should be out of date.
– Taiichi Ohno, the "father" of the Toyota production system.

Much has been written about the "two pillars" of the Toyota production system – just-in-time and autonomation – designed by the late Taiichi Ohno. Although this remarkable combination played a large role in creating the efficiency and success of the Toyota Motor Company, these technological breakthroughs aren't the whole story. The fine-tuning that made the Toyota production system really work came not from upper management, nor from the engineers, but from the shop floor in the form of employee suggestions – over 20 million ideas in the last 40 years.

The Toyota Creative Idea suggestion system evolved hand in hand with Ohno's vision for a rationalized, efficient automobile plant. One of his basic tenets was to question assumptions and "conventional wisdom," to continually ask *why*. He saw the need not only for a top-down strategy to drive toward specific goals, but also for a bottom-up movement of individual workers and teams to make creative improvements and eliminate wasteful activities.

The Prologue of journalist Yuzo Yasuda's *40 Years, 20 Million Ideas* sets the stage for the Toyota suggestion system story. He begins with a provocative comparison between the participation-oriented suggestion system that has developed in Japan and the image that comes to most Americans' minds when they hear "suggestion system" – a dusty, locked box that no one pays any real attention to.

Yasuda here explores a key element behind the widespread success of the participative-type system: its first priority is not to save or make a lot of money, but to involve workers in improving the management of the company business. This approach produces fundamentally different results, creating a company culture in which people can work together harmoniously and experience personal satisfaction.

Chapter One of the book describes the philosophy of the Toyota Creative Idea suggestion system and the organizational structure that supports it. The critical nature of visible, active top management involvement, not merely support, is driven home throughout the book. At Toyota, senior management officials serve in the top positions of the Creative Idea Suggestion System Committee, which oversees policy and evaluates high-scoring proposals.

This first chapter also describes the evaluation process in some detail. The importance of management support for employee ideas is borne out by such practices as supervisors helping employees try out suggestions on the shop floor before they are submitted for evaluation. Managers also formally present their employees' high-scoring ideas for an audience of the company's senior management.

Chapter Two traces the origins of the Toyota Creative Idea suggestion system – an idea originally witnessed at the Ford River Rouge plant by Toyota's top officers in 1949 and since transformed into a system that expresses the Toyota Motor culture.

A unique feature of the Toyota suggestion system, an employee group called the Good Idea (GI) Club, grew from an ad hoc social gathering of top suggestion writers into a grassroots organization that conducts suggestion-writing training and educational exchanges throughout the company. The history and methods of the GI Club are described in Chapter Three.

Chapter Four presents ten examples of suggestions submitted from various parts of the company, including administrative divisions. (The book draws attention to some of the special issues of conducting improvement programs in white-collar areas, where work traditionally is seen as difficult to measure.)

In Chapter Five, the author returns to the philosophy of the Toyota company as a key to understanding the role of individual creative effort within the company.

40 Years, 20 Million Ideas is valuable for its wealth of information about the inner workings of one of the world's most productive suggestion programs in one of the most successful global competitors of the decade. Any company serious about attaining a leading position in the expanding world marketplace has something to learn and to implement from the example. The tools are available – *The Idea Book*, (Productivity Press, 1988) and *The Service Industry Idea Book* (Productivity Press, 1990) provide working references for implementing a companywide suggestion program. We encourage you to read these books and think about how these ideas can give your company an edge in the international era that is upon us. And then *do* something.

We would like to thank Kazuya Uchiyama, Assistant Director of the Publication and Information Development Division of the Japan Management Association, for the privilege of producing this book in English. Thanks also to Toshio Sugihara, Editor of the Publication and Information Division of the Japan Management Association, for his assistance in answering questions about the translation.

We appreciate the work of Steven Ott, Vice President of Productivity Press, for arranging for the publication of this English edition. We are especially grateful to Steve Ansuini, Suggestion System Coordinator of the Toyota Motor Manufacturing plant in Georgetown, Kentucky, for his insightful foreword and other assistance in clarifying concepts within the book.

This manuscript was translated by Fred Czupryna, with in-house assistance from Sally Schwager and Mugi Hanao. Karen Jones managed the developmental edit, and Marie Cantlon was managing editor for Dana Wilson (copyediting) and Danny Marcus, (proofreading). David Lennon managed production of the book, which was typeset by the staff of Rudra Press, Cambridge, Massachusetts.

Norman Bodek
President
Productivity, Inc.

Preface

The Toyota Motor Company first began to attract attention for its high profitability in 1973, after the oil crisis. That was the year when Japan's economy changed from the high growth it had experienced until then to a low-growth situation. Toyota stood out because it boasted high profits despite such an economic environment.

The Toyota production system was praised as the driving force behind Toyota's strength. But the more Toyota's strength was emphasized, the more its image congealed as a company whose employees were mere cogs in the Toyota production machine, without individual identity, members of a group that suppressed individuality. But was this really a fair picture of the company? My interest in that question continued for a long time.

One day an article caught my attention as I was reading the *Toyota News*, an in-house journal issued by the Toyota Public Relations Division, which I receive regularly. The title of that 1988 article was "Total Number of Creative Idea Suggestions Over 20 Million." The article pointed out that in the 37 years since its beginning in 1951, more than 20 million suggestions had been made.

But what interested me more than that were the following lines explaining the meaning of the creative idea suggestion system:

> *The creative idea suggestion system is not limited to techni-*
> *cal and manufacturing improvements. All employees can sug-*
> *gest their ideas spontaneously whenever they want.*
> *Suggesting their ideas helps all employees to be aware that*
> *they are participating in management. Besides the effect this*
> *system has on making the workplace more dynamic, it also has*
> *a very significant effect on improving management.*

If Toyota were really trying to suppress the individuality of its employees, they would not be involved in spontaneous creative idea suggestion activities. But is the participation of Toyota employees in this system really spontaneous? The answer to this question should definitely show us the Toyota company as it really is.

While mulling over such thoughts, I began to gather material. No sooner had I begun than I heard statements such as, "What it really boils down to is that I want to make my job easier to do, even if only a little easier. So that's why I throw myself so completely into suggestion activities." Perhaps employees participate in creative idea suggestion activities because of such human desires. These human desires seemed to be the spirit that supports the creative idea suggestion system.

I wondered if it wouldn't be possible to present a vivid description of the human spirit supporting this system by showing the structure of the creative idea suggestion system and by gathering material from various employees who were participating in suggestion activities at the workplace. I felt that by doing these things the real Toyota would emerge, plain and clear for all to see. Nothing would make me happier than to have my vantage point perceived by the reader, and I hope that the reader will be helped in some way by this book about the creative idea suggestion activities which may be called one of the little known driving forces behind one of the leading companies of Japan. This book is also about the GI (Good Idea) Club, an independent activities circle that grew out of creative idea suggestion activities.

I want to thank all those who helped in the writing of this book in spite of my disruptions of their work schedules. I am grateful to many people in the Public Relations Division and the Toyota Creative Idea Committee Secretariat for helping me gather material. I want to thank journalist Takayuki Yamamoto for helping me to collect material. I also want to express my gratitude to Toshio Sugiwara and Kengo Honda, of the Japan Management Association Publications Editing Division, for vigorously spurring me on.

Yuzo Yasuda

40 Years,
20 Million Ideas

The Toyota Suggestion System

Prologue

Making Improvements Is the Key to Japan's Industrial Strength

"If the yen gets any stronger, I won't be able to survive."

With the rapid appreciation of the yen after the 1985 Group of Five meeting, the myth that Japanese manufactured goods nevertheless would sell was fundamentally destroyed. Cries of pain from Japan's captains of industry could be heard all over the country. Some felt that in planning to make the dollar weaker and yen stronger, the U.S. government meant to weaken Japanese companies, and many thought that this objective would be easily attained.

Most Japanese companies, however, showed a characteristic ability to adjust by thorough rationalization and other means. Moving from dependence on foreign demand to a situation of stimulating domestic demand, they skillfully met the challenge of Japan's economic structural change and somehow managed to avoid a crisis.

A foreign economics journal put together a special edition that observed more and more rationalization in Japanese industry. It praised Japan for its toughness in this "third Japanese economic miracle" (after the post-war economic recovery and the handling of the oil crises). Most of Japan's media were also proclaiming that the yen was too strong. In spite of that, however, they could not conceal their true feeling of relief that Japan's economy had reached its limits.

But just why was it that Japan's industry had become so strong? While foreign companies were losing out to Japanese companies in global economic competition, the key to understanding this phenomenon was considered from various perspectives under the rubric of "Japanese-style management." But no one could give a complete explanation.

Before long, however, a single concept became popular as it shocked the business world and made the world begin to understand a fundamental concept of Japanese-style management. That concept is "continuous improvement" (*kaizen*).

Today, everyone knows the word kaizen – the Japanese word is used around the world without being translated. Ironically, however, the company "improvement systems" and "creative idea systems" that support improvement activities were originally imported from the United States, like so much other technology and manufactured goods.

Eastman Kodak, an American company, is said to have been the first company to receive a suggestion, in 1898. The content of that suggestion was to wash the windows in order to make the workplace brighter. Viewed from our current perspective, this was amazingly simple and not something that technically could be called an improvement. As of 1975, the Kodak company had recorded 800,260 suggestions and the total amount of cash awards paid out during those 78 years is said to have reached $1,620,000.

In Japan, a suggestion system and suggestion box were set up at the Kanebo company in 1905, after the company's managers returned from a trip to the United States, where they observed the NCR company's suggestion system. Apart from this suggestion box, the only Japanese companies that had introduced suggestion systems before World War II were Hitachi in 1930, Yasukawa Electric in 1932 and Origin Electric in 1938. So the history of suggestion systems in Japan, which has achieved an unparalleled level of prosperity, only began after World War II.

The first major period in the establishment of suggestion systems in Japan was during the early 1950s. Toyota Motor Company and other companies using modern suggestion systems accounted for about 7 percent of all Japanese companies. That was the launching period for introducing suggestion systems.

Later, they were put on the same track with QC (Quality Control) circle activities. The second major period was from the mid-1950s to the mid-1960s. During that period, manufacturing companies had almost completed the introduction of suggestion systems. In the third period, from the mid-1970s to the mid-1980s, suggestion systems spread also to non-manufacturing industries such as the distribution industry, financial institutions, retail stores, and the like.

Why the American-style Suggestion System Declined

Although the nearly 40-year-old Japanese suggestion system was originally based on the American suggestion system, it now has a uniquely Japanese-style structure.

The American system was strongly influenced by the values of individualism and cost-consciousness (awareness of the value in making suggestions). The American-style system encouraged "professional thinkers," a concept unfamiliar to Japanese companies, which considered group concerns much more important than individual concerns.

The traditional American-style suggestion system tends to "buy" the ideas of some of the company's gifted individuals. The evaluation of those ideas is based entirely on how much monetary benefit will be contributed to the company. This means that the foundation of the system is to pay out the equivalent of 10 percent of the economic efficiency generated by the ideas.

In the Japanese suggestion system, on the other hand, because the employees responsible for the workplace have a thorough knowledge of their jobs, they are constantly making improvements in their work and actively considering how they can create a work environment that will make jobs easier to do. There is almost none of what Americans call "cost-consciousness" involved in this.

According to a 1987 survey by the National Association of Suggestion Systems (a North American organization that promotes suggestion systems), American companies that had introduced a suggestion system had an 8 percent participation rate; that is, only 8 out of 100 employees made one suggestion each year. Cash awards for each suggestion used amounted to $605 (at a ¥130/dollar exchange rate, this comes to ¥78,650) and the amount of economic efficiency achieved per suggestion was $8000 (or ¥1,040,000).

In contrast, the Japanese participation rate averaged 67 percent. Fifty percent of the Japanese companies had participation rates higher than 90 percent, supporting the perception of Japanese society as group oriented. Furthermore, the amount of cash award per suggestion used was ¥423 ($3.25), 1/186th of the comparable amount given at the time in the United States. The economic benefit per suggestion was ¥18,000 ($138), 1/58th of the comparable American amount.

Conspicuous differences between the Japanese and American systems are evident even in the statistics. This obviously does not mean that there are no Japanese companies with suggestion systems resembling the American style. For example, Tohoku Oki Electric Company is an enterprise with almost 880 employees eligible to make suggestions, but the cash award amount per person per year is ¥190,000 ($1400.)

and the economic benefit generated is reported to be ¥4,840,000 ($37,000), indicating that this company has a superior suggestion system. When these figures are compared with the Japanese national average of a ¥8088 ($62) cash award per person, they show that this company has reached a level two or three times the average, and has achieved an economic benefit that is 88 times higher than average. (The overall average among Japanese companies is ¥55,000 ($423).)

There are also examples of companies like Ohita Canon, which boasts cash awards of ¥10,000 and ¥20,000 ($75 and $150) per person, with economic benefits of ¥1,680,000 ($13,000). But there are two decisive reasons why the suggestion systems at both of these enterprises are not traditional American-style systems, despite such statistics.

First of all, the suggestion participation rate at both companies has reached 100 percent. Second, while the number of suggestions per person in the United States is at best only 0.13, the comparable figures are 1275 for Tohoku Oki Electric and 656 for Ohita Canon. These figures reveal Japan's unique strong points in its high volume suggestion system.*

"Wringing a Dry Towel Even Drier"

It seems that the more severe the economic environment, the less people talk about things like creative ideas. On the other hand, however, many leading Japanese companies strongly assert that the suggestion system is one of the main pillars of management.

The Japan Human Relations Association (JHRA) notes that some Japanese companies place so much importance on

---

* The statistics on Japanese company suggestion systems were compiled by the Japan Human Relations Association (JHRA), a national organization that promotes suggestion system activities in Japanese companies.

suggestion-writing that each job is assigned a fixed quota to produce, and managers and assistant managers can be penalized when those quotas are not met.

Some would criticize companies that exercise centralized power that way, and such companies are somewhat abnormal. But at the opposite end of the spectrum, some companies still do not fully understand the importance of suggestion systems.

> *Every year we get requests for detailed information about our company's suggestion system. But when the request is made by phone and the other party's position is only a middle manager or a lower-level executive, we can only apologize for giving a mere outline of basic facts, and for declining to give any information beyond that.*

The person who said this is a subsection manager in the secretariat of the Toyota Motor Company Creative Idea Committee. He does not mean that serious inquiries must be handled by the president of the other company in person, but it does mean that someone at a level of responsibility equivalent to that of the caller should handle such inquiries. People have various opinions about this policy, but one thing that emerges clearly is the significant status of the Toyota suggestion system within the company.

There are actually some interesting data involved here relating to upper management involvement in Japanese suggestion systems. The JHRA surveyed 649 companies and enterprises throughout Japan to learn the company titles of the people with the most responsibility for suggestion activities.

The results showed that 48.2 percent of all the companies involved had people in top management positions occupying the most responsible positions in suggestion systems. More specifically, in those companies with more than 5000 employees, 51.5 percent had appointed members of the board (including 10.3 percent who appointed company presidents). At companies with less than 5000 but more than 1000 employees, the percentage appointing board members was 45.2 percent. At companies with fewer than 1000 but more than 500 employees, the percentage was 29.7 percent. In other words, people in very high-level management positions were being appointed to the highest positions of responsibility in suggestion systems in a significant percentage of all the companies regardless of their size. Although it may not be well known, the challenges of suggestion activities are not at all limited to private enterprise. The Postal Service, for example, has to compete for home mail delivery, a situation which has spread to prefectural offices in Shizuoka, Niigata, and other places.

As suggestion activities have become more active, doubtful or scrutinizing reactions toward suggestion systems have also become more conspicuous. Even some famous economists have expressed opinions that "independent activities" are a euphemism that conceals the reality of using coercion on the labor force or that the activities are "totalitarian and fascist."

Toyota is typical of companies forced to stand these attacks. It is common knowledge that Toyota produces vehicles of comparable quality more cheaply than its competitors because of its thorough production control system. This cost reduction is based on the Toyota production system and on its Creative Idea Suggestion System. This has resulted in occasional backbiting, sometimes expressed as "wringing a dry towel even drier."

But is the criticism of Toyota valid? While I was attending a year-end party to collect material for this book, one Toyota worker who had had a few drinks gave the following stinging response on behalf of his fellow employees: "Wringing a dry towel drier? Come on, you've got to be kidding. That expression doesn't do justice to the efforts we make to reduce costs. We should not make a fuss over that expression. At any rate, it's not something that happens simply by commanding subordinates to do it!"

The Creative Idea Suggestion System, one of the two main supports for this cost reduction, began its growth period around 1974, the year the GI (Good Idea) Club was begun (Chapter 3 deals more specifically with this employee group). The vigorous activities of this autonomous activities circle contributed independently to opportunities related to suggestion activities among individual employees. This, in fact, was not a matter of managers giving commands to workers.

What are the results of employees at the workplace being motivated to deal with the challenge of cost control? Let's consider here something that happened to Nissan, one of Toyota's competitors. Since April 1986, when Nissan normalized relations with its workers following a period of adversarial labor relations, the company began to take the initiative in vigorously accepting the challenges of rationalization. Before then, it had an authoritarian centralized policy in which company headquarters issued orders to each factory explaining its cost objectives and its cost-reduction policy. But a consensus emerged that there would be no real and effective cost reductions unless workplaces acted independently.

After considering cost reduction methods to be applied independently at each factory and workplace, a system was adopted to encourage mutual competition. Consequently, efficiency improvement activities progressed smoothly in areas such as productivity and cost reduction. The cost reduction in fiscal 1986 greatly exceeded initial objectives, and labor costs were reduced by 20 percent.

Total cost reductions amounted to more than ¥100 billion ($750 million). At factories alone, a ¥50 billion ($375 million) cost reduction was achieved, almost twice as much as the objective of ¥30 billion ($225 million).

Despite this success, some doubt remained about why suggestion activities that did not produce profits should be continued. The reason is closely related to the corporate culture and values. These activities are the secret behind the strength and high profits of Japanese companies.

This book focuses on Toyota Motor Company, which some believe to have the most effective suggestion system.In light of the company's great financial success, we hope to probe deeply into its Creative Idea Suggestion System and the role of the GI Club in support of those activities

CHAPTER ONE

The Secrets of Toyota's Successful Suggestion System

Creative Ideas to Make Work Easier

"I want to make my work easier to do, even if only a little bit easier." This is the spirit behind the Toyota Motor Company's Creative Idea Suggestion System. This is a very human desire and it seems to be part of the foundation supporting this suggestion system. Why participate in Creative Idea suggestion activities? The answer to this question reveals how employees involved in suggestion activities really feel about them.

From an employee's perspective, the purpose is to make one's job easier. From the company's perspective, the purposes are to increase the skill of employees who make suggestions by increasing their problem consciousness and implementing their suggestions, and to use suggestion activities to build a workplace environment where it is easy to work.

These ideas may seem a bit too formal, but they coincide with the feelings of the Toyota employees who participate in suggestion activities. A third purpose flows logically from them: to contribute to the expansion and structural improvement of the company. This point is actually the result of the first two points, which are always the major objectives of carrying out Creative Idea suggestion activities.

The concrete objectives of the Creative Idea Suggestion System are shown in Figure 1-1. It is clear from this table that creative ideas facilitate "environment building" so that jobs can be done more comfortably. But better environment building cannot be achieved by doing one's job in an aimless manner. Aren't there ways to do one's work more comfortably, accurately, quickly, inexpensively, and safely? The Creative Idea suggestion program encourages constant problem consciousness corresponding to each item shown in the table. This will result in the improvement of those problem points that are detected. This is the meaning of a creative idea.

It is easy to talk about things such as problem consciousness, but achieving it is difficult. What should be done to make problems detectable? Consider the possibility of any irrationality, waste, or inconsistency in one's job with respect to each item listed as an objective in Figure 1-1. For example, can wasteful walking be reduced by even one second? Or can a posture that makes a worker tire easily be made at least a little bit more comfortable? Trouble results from continuing the feelings of tension that come from these kinds of wasteful movements or unnatural postures. These things unavoidably result in work inconsistencies. People who are looking for problems of irrationality, waste, and inconsistency will certainly have problem consciousness.

It is important to create an environment in which problems are easily detected. Toyota uses the term *5S* for its basic industrial housekeeping methods: arranging things, putting them in order, neatness, cleaning, and discipline.* If each

---

* "5S" refers to the initials of the five Japanese words for these concepts. Some work areas refer to the first four of these elements as "4S."

worker implements each of these points thoroughly, any problems of waste or inconsistency will become clearly visible. If people are on the alert to detect problem points, and if an environment is created that makes it easy to notice problems, the supply of creative idea "seeds" will not run out.

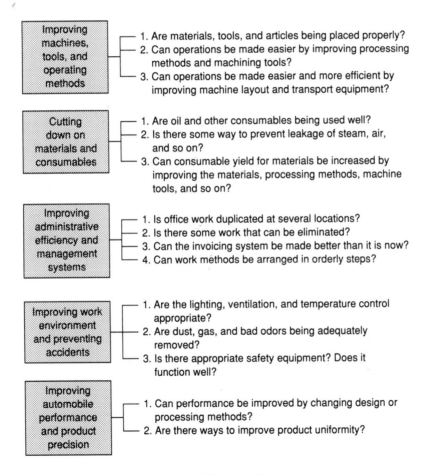

Improving machines, tools, and operating methods
1. Are materials, tools, and articles being placed properly?
2. Can operations be made easier by improving processing methods and machining tools?
3. Can operations be made easier and more efficient by improving machine layout and transport equipment?

Cutting down on materials and consumables
1. Are oil and other consumables being used well?
2. Is there some way to prevent leakage of steam, air, and so on?
3. Can consumable yield for materials be increased by improving the materials, processing methods, machine tools, and so on?

Improving administrative efficiency and management systems
1. Is office work duplicated at several locations?
2. Is there some work that can be eliminated?
3. Can the invoicing system be made better than it is now?
4. Can work methods be arranged in orderly steps?

Improving work environment and preventing accidents
1. Are the lighting, ventilation, and temperature control appropriate?
2. Are dust, gas, and bad odors being adequately removed?
3. Is there appropriate safety equipment? Does it function well?

Improving automobile performance and product precision
1. Can performance be improved by changing design or processing methods?
2. Are there ways to improve product uniformity?

Figure 1-1. Concrete Examples of Creative Ideas

Asking "Why" Again and Again
Until Basic Causes Are Found

After a problem has been detected, the next things that must be done are to ask why this problem has occurred and then to search for its causes. Asking why the problem occurred must be repeated until the underlying cause is found. If the search for causes is only perfunctory, creative ideas will be based on mistaken assessments, and in some cases there will be no improvement but rather retrogression.

The following is a case in point. This story is about a distribution center at which many trucks were loaded and unloaded in the afternoon. Vehicles were parked outside the area constantly, and there was continual trouble in the neighborhood. The problem here was that there were too many trucks at the distribution center. What was the cause of that situation?

The results of a study showed that the space at the distribution center was too small and that there were not enough platforms for the trucks to pull up to. Assuming that those were the causes, it would be simple to make improvements. An improvement suggestion was submitted right away, proposing an expansion of distribution center space and the construction of more platforms.

There were some employees, however, who had some doubts and wondered whether there might be a different reason for the large number of trucks, so they began to investigate what those causes might be. This led them to realize that the reason for the crowding of so many trucks at the distribution center was that the trucks that had pulled up to the platforms had to wait a long time. When they tried to find out why things took such a long time, they realized it was because the merchandise was not ready right away. The reason the merchandise wasn't ready right away finally emerged after their examination. The merchandise was not ready because work had been allocated in such a way that separate merchandise groups were arranged separately by floors.

Changes were made by having different loading routes for work teams dealing with each floor and each merchandise group. This immediately shortened the waiting time for the trucks and solved the crowding problem, avoiding the need to construct any additional platforms.

If it had been assumed that the basic cause was that the distribution center space was too small, and additional platforms had been constructed to improve that situation, the crowding problem would not have been solved. At best, the waiting time would have been made just a bit shorter than before. On the negative side, the amount of money spent to construct additional platforms would have produced only a slight degree of improvement. This is a good example of why it is necessary to probe deeply into basic causes.

Toyota gives the following advice to its employees for investigating basic causes:

> *When struggling to solve some problem, gather as many facts as possible that are related to it to get a solid grasp of the nature of the problem. After the information has been gathered, it must be collated and put into a form that is immediately comprehensible. Especially when coping with deep-rooted problems in cases of group suggestions, using drawings helps to clarify problem points and to unify the mutual problem consciousness of group members involved. Also, when workplace problems are meticulously analyzed to this extent, it leads to the detection of countless improvement objectives.*

5W2H: The Key to the Toyota Method of Inspiring Ideas

After a cause has been understood, the next thing to do is to decide how to solve the problem that stems from that cause. At that point, it is no exaggeration to say that the way countermeasures are devised from various perspectives will determine the quality of the improvement suggestions.

For example, let's assume that changing the position of something from right to left will make work easier to do. A solution has been found, but rather than being satisfied at that point, one should try to think more deeply about the problem. What about suspending the object? Or getting rid of it? Every situation should be considered to that extent.

Of course, there are times when such ideas are simply not forthcoming, so Toyota developed its own method of inspiring ideas, which is called 5W2H. Figure 1-2 shows the elements of this method.

The first two W's refer to what and why, ideas involving the elimination of any aspects of a job that are not necessary. The next three W's refer to Where, When, and Who – ways to inspire ideas for changing combinations or sequences. The ideas of How and How Much help in the selection of improvement methods. Countermeasures for improvement are devised based on this assessment of the situation.

When implementation seems feasible, efforts are made to make things even more efficient. No matter how creative or attractive an idea is, if it does not produce much efficiency, or seems inferior to other ideas, it should be rejected at that stage. If an idea seems too attractive to reject completely, however, it should be retained and reflected on again and again; there may be ways it can be modified to produce greater efficiency. There are many ideas that have been beautifully restored to life in this way. In some cases, greater efficiency can come from combining several ideas rather than by trying to milk one idea dry.

Something else that must be considered in the implementation of a new idea is how to deal with situations when the improvement changes relationships between other operations or other processes. This is also an important factor that must be taken into account when trying to come up with ideas.

Ideas are recognized and rewarded by the Creative Idea committee according to the criteria listed in Figure 1-3. An awareness of these criteria helps those who make suggestions to get the most out of their ideas.

The Creative Idea Committee: Members and Functions

The Creative Idea committee functions as a screening system to evaluate suggestions from QC circle-type small groups

WHAT (object)	What is being done? Can this work be eliminated?
WHY (purpose)	Why is that work necessary? Clarify its purpose
WHERE (location)	Where is it being done? Does it have to be done there?
WHEN (sequence)	When is the best time to do it? Does it have to be done then?
WHO (people)	Who is doing it? Would it be better to have someone else do it? Why am I doing this?
HOW (method)	How is it being done? Is this the best way to do it? Are there other ways of doing it?
HOW MUCH (cost)	How much does it cost now? How much will it cost to improve?

Figure 1-2. How to Think about 5W2H

Benefits of implementation (degree of contribution to management goals)

1. Tangible benefits: Benefits that can be measured financially, such as increased revenue, improved productivity, reduced number of employees needed for a particular job, shorter time required, reduced amount of materials, reduced labor-hours, and so on.
2. Intangible efficiency: Benefits that cannot be measured financially, such as quality, delivery dates, safety, hygiene, orderly arrangement of the workplace, labor reduction, increased morale, improved human relations, improved work rules, improved company image, increased customer confidence, and so on.

Feasibility (difficulty of implementation)

The actual money and time required; the level or urgency to implement (should implementation be immediate or gradual?).

Applicability (scope)

Whether the ideas in the suggestion can be used at other work areas in the company.

Effects on others

Whether the implementation of the suggestion would have any bad influence on other workplaces or processes.

Continuity

Whether the benefits of the suggestion are long lasting or temporary.

Completeness

Whether the suggestion is concrete enough to implement immediately without modification or additional work.

Originality

Whether the idea is original and creative, a clever adaptation of someone else's idea, or simply an imitation of a prior idea.

Research effort

The amount of research, trial and error, and other efforts expended by the suggester. Was the suggestion just a passing thought or does it represent adversities overcome through courage and effort?

Work demerits

What is the relationship between the suggestion and the suggester's position? What effort was spent in the suggestion relative to the suggester's abilities?

Figure 1-3. Idea Evaluation Criteria

or from individual employees, using the evaluation criteria. This committee also manages the Creative Idea Suggestion System and vigorously promotes suggestion activities. It is the highest authoritative Creative Idea Suggestion System.

This committee is composed of a chairman (senior managing director rank, or higher), a vice-chairman (managing director rank, or higher), and committee members of the rank of director or general manager. The current committee chairman is Tatsuro Toyoda, vice president of the company, and the vice-chairman is Toshimi Onishi, the senior managing director.

The importance Toyota attaches to its Creative Idea Suggestion System is evident in its selection of such top management people to lead the committee. Since this system was introduced in 1951, there have been seven committee chairmen. The first was Shoichi Saito (then a senior managing director), the second was Shoichiro Toyoda (also a senior managing director), the third was Taiichi Ohno (then a company vice-president), the fourth was Toshio Morita (then company vice-president), the fifth was Shigeru Aoki (then senior managing director), the sixth was Kaneyoshi Kusunoki (another company vice-president), and the seventh is the current chairman. An outstanding lineup indeed.

Creative Idea committee vice-chairman Onishi said the following about the role of vice-chairman: "As a result of involvement during suggestion activities, there are some workplaces that reach a mature phase and others that remain in a growing stage. The vice-chairman has to look at the whole picture, checking on whether workplace levels differ in terms of suggestion content or number of suggestions, as well as on what the reasons are for such differences in level."

Those with the greatest responsibility for managing the Creative Idea Suggestion System must be people with considerable authority within the company so that they will have a solid grasp of the situation from the perspective of the whole company in regard to the Creative Idea suggestion activities. This will help them to orient these activities more effectively. That is why people in top management positions are made the chairman and vice-chairman of the Creative Idea committee.

The Pyramid-shaped Organization Supporting the Suggestion System

Suggestion systems are now being introduced by many companies, and more companies are planning to introduce them in the future. Companies that plan to introduce suggestion systems in the future have a good model in the Toyota Creative Idea Suggestion System, which has increased the company's performance since its early introduction. Requests pour in to the Creative Idea committee secretariat, or administrative office, for information about the suggestion system content and management methods because of the strong desire to learn from Toyota's example.

Shinro Haneda and Tsuyoshi Bando, who contributed for a long time to the promotion of Creative Idea suggestion activities as members of this secretariat, insist that the success of these activities depends on the sympathetic understanding of top management. Haneda, forcing a smile, said: "Companies asking for information generally want to contact the secretariat at company headquarters, but some people have a lot of nerve. There were even people who asked us to telephone them, because they were located in remote areas, and then to send them the information later. But we decline to give explanations to people making these kinds of inquiries. After all, it is really impossible to explain such things on the telephone."

Nor is everything explained to representatives of companies who actually come to visit Toyota headquarters. As Bando put it:

Just who are these people coming to visit us? Usually they are managers at levels similar to those of our (Toyota's)

Creative Idea secretariat people. But when the people who are in positions equivalent to that of the chairman of Toyota's Creative Idea committee are only middle managers or low-level executives in their companies, our initial discussion does not go beyond generalities. This gives us a chance to learn how the management of those companies thinks about suggestion activities. If people at a lower level of responsibility are put charge of suggestion activities, they will never be able to cope with suggestion activities on a company-wide basis. The people responsible for managing suggestion systems must be top management people with authority throughout the company; otherwise there will be no positive results no matter how much they listen to explanations and adopt these systems.

Toyota does give serious advice, however, to companies that appear willing to improve their organization and cope with suggestion activities or if they are already coping with them. For example, take the case of the Nada Kobe Cooperative. It has been 10 years since the introduction of a suggestion system by the Nada Kobe Cooperative, but results have not been as good as expected. Some representatives visited the Toyota secretariat to study its Creative Idea Suggestion System. After hearing about the situation of the Cooperative's suggestion activities, various specific deficiencies came to light: they do not have a system that allows those making suggestions to function autonomously, and there are problems with their suggestion evaluation methods, to name two. They were given advice on improvement measures they could take to deal with these areas. The Cooperative is now using this advice in studying how to make fundamental revisions in its suggestion system.

There are 18 plant and division committees organized under the Creative Idea committee (see Figure 1-4). Each of these committees is composed of a committee chair (plant director, board member in charge of division) and committee members (general manager or assistant general manager of each division). Each also has a secretariat. The roles of the plant and division committees are to promote Creative Idea activities within the plants and divisions and to deliberate and report on matters submitted for consideration by the Creative Idea committee chairman.

There are also subcommittees below the factory and division committees. They are composed of directing committee members (general managers), committee members (section managers from each section), and other managers very well informed about a division's work. Their roles are to promote Creative Idea suggestion activities by subcommittees and to deliberate and report on matters submitted for consideration by plant and division committee chairmen. Plant and division committees as well as subcommittees play a screening role in regard to suggestions.

The Meticulously Organized
Suggestion Screening System

What kind of screening is done by the Creative Idea committee, the plant and division committees, and the subcommittees of those suggestions that are submitted? Before we consider the screening system, there must be an explanation of the cash awards that are so important in the Creative Idea Suggestion System.

The suggestions received from employees (both from individuals and from groups) are ranked according to quality of suggestion, that is, according to the evaluation criteria listed in Figure 1-3. Cash awards are decided according to that ranking, and then given to the employees who have made the suggestions.

Suggestions submitted by employees are screened on the same day by their immediate managers (factory managers, heads of subsections, or those generally referred to as

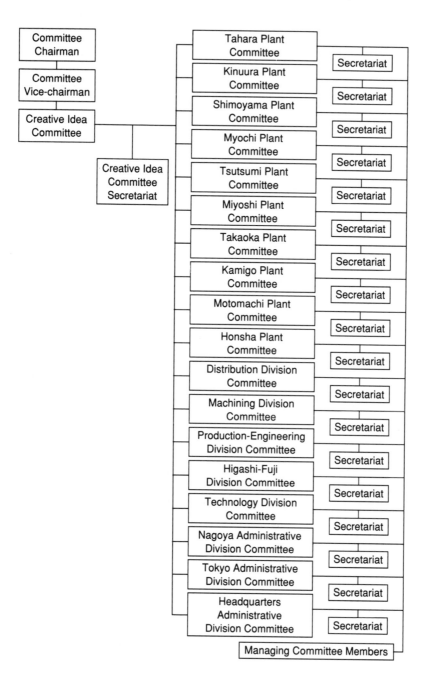

Figure 1-4. The Creative Idea Committee Review Organization

foremen) and given to the subcommittees. The outstanding suggestions among those that are received are evaluated as "superior" on the basis of the criteria previously described. More specifically, points are used to indicate various levels of benefit:

Tangible benefit	0 - 20 points
Intangible benefit	0 - 20 points

Points are also used to indicate how outstanding the idea is or how much effort went into it:

Adaptability	0 - 5 points
Creativity	0 - 10 points
Originality	0 - 10 points
Effort	0 - 10 points

An overall evaluation is based on the total number of points for these factors. "Work" and "investment" points (demerits) are subtracted from the total of these evaluation points on the basis of the degree of relationship to the original job or how much money will have to be spent for the improvement. The final number of evaluation points for a suggestion is determined after work points and investment points are subtracted from the total number of evaluation points. Figure 1-5 shows the scoring system.

The cash award amounts are decided according to the final number of evaluation points. For those suggestions that are evaluated by subcommittee screening as deserving awards of ¥5000 ($40) or less, this decision is final. Those suggestions that are evaluated by subcommittees as deserving awards of ¥6000 ($45) or more are considered "superior" suggestions and are sent for screening by factory and division committees. After screening by factory and division committees, suggestions that receive cash awards ranging from ¥6000 to ¥10,500 ($45 to $80) are finalized at this point. Suggestions

Award Money Criteria

Points received		equivalent to																										
	C 0-4	B 5-7	A 8-9	10-11	12-14	15-17	18-20	21-23	24-26	27-29	30-32	33-35	36-38	39-41	42-44	45-46	47-48	49-50	51-52	53-54	55-56	57-58	59-61	62-64	65-67	68-70	71-73	74-75
Award money (10,000s of yen)	none	.05	.10	.20	.30	.40	.50	.60	.80	1.0	1.5	2.0	3.0	4.0	5.0	6.0	8.0	10.0	11.0	12.0	13.0	14.0	15.0	16.0	17.0	18.0	19.0	20.0

Creative Idea Evaluation Score Table

Benefit A (numeric thresholds)

Cost reduction (10,000s of yen/month)	0 / no benefit, then: <1.5, 1.5, 3, 5.5, 8, 12, 16, 24, 28, 35, 42, 50, 58, 67, 76, 86, 96, 109, 121, 150 or more
Personnel reduction (number of persons)	no benefit, then: 1, 2, 3 or more

Benefit B (numeric thresholds)

Equipment investment reduction (10,000s of yen/month)	0 / no benefit, then: <1.5, 1.5, 3, 5.5, 8, 12, 16, 24, 28, 35, 42, 50, 58, 67, 76, 86, 96, 109, 121, 150 or more
Labor-hour reduction (hours/month)	0 / no benefit, then: 1, 10, 30, 50, 70, 100, 130, 160, 200, 250, 300 or more
Labor-hour/personnel reduction (hours/month)	0 / no benefit, then: 1, 55, 110 or more

Benefit B (descriptive criteria, levels 0–5)

Level	0	1	2	3	4	5
Space saved (m²)	less than prescribed	100 exterior / 50 interior / 25 office	200 exterior / 100 interior / 50 office	300 exterior / 150 interior / 75 office	400 exterior / 200 interior / 100 office	500 exterior / 250 interior / 125 office
Safety	safer than before	safety maintained without extra effort	careless accidents prevented	extra safety precautions taken to prevent trouble	safety maintained mechanically (without human attention)	safety maintained in any kind of situation
Hygiene (environmental conditions)	no efficiency	environment improved; operation became easier	improved to the extent that it is not unpleasant; operations that cause fatigue are eliminated	troublesome environment improved; unnatural posture eliminated	workplace environment made more pleasant; stressful operations that had to be done in half-shifts are eliminated	created a superb environment that did not exist before; environment was improved or operations eliminated to a degree surpassing ordinary standards
Quality (excluding quantitative)	—	product quality maintained or improved	occurrence of defects eliminated	defects eliminated; checks no longer necessary	quality and reliability improved; inspection eliminated	product value increased; company image improved
Other	—	slightly significant benefit	fairly significant benefit	significant benefit	benefit	extraordinary benefit
Adaptability	none	can be used within section	can be used extensively within division	can be used for same type of processing both at own factory and at other factories (suppliers)	can be widely used throughout the whole company, including diverse types of processing	wide range of applicability, both for whole company and for suppliers
Creativity	none	good because hints from others were applied	applicable and feasible; quite creative	excellent idea and means of implementing it; rather creative (can be submitted as an implementable new suggestion)	excellent idea and means of implementing it; very creative (patent application possible)	excellent idea and means of implementing it; extraordinarily creative (patent application possible)
Originality	none	good originality because of hints from others	significant observation of troublesome problems	good observation of neglected daily problem	excellent idea for solving major problem left untouched for a long time	extraordinary idea for dealing with major problem noticed by no one else for a long time
Effort	none	made efforts	worked hard to implement; made fairly strong efforts	worked hard for a long time to implement; made strong efforts	worked very hard and made very strong efforts to overcome all problems involving implementation	hard work and effort at an extraordinary level in overcoming adverse circumstances

- **Work demerits** (percentage reduction for suggestions related to one's own job)
- **Demerits for line employees with technical ability**

	Suggestions made by foremen and group leaders · Suggestions made by general employees with technical ability related to improving their jobs · Joint suggestions made by foremen and group leaders together with general employees with technical ability and those mentioned above	+	Suggestions made by foreman and group leaders related to improving their jobs · Joint suggestions made by foreman and group leaders together with general employees with technical ability, related to improving their jobs	Involving administrative and technical workers in implementation — Worker received advice	Involving administrative and technical workers in implementation — Worker received cooperation or assistance
Subject					
%	10%		20%	10%	20%

Demerits for administrative and technical staff

Subject	Suggestion almost entirely related to own job	Suggestion substantially related to own job	Suggestion somewhat related to own job
%	50% or more	30-40%	20%

Figure 1-5. Creative Idea Suggestion Evaluation Score Criteria Table

Award Money Criteria — equivalent to

Points received	C 0-4	B 5-7	A 8-9	10-11	12-14	15-17	18-20	21-23	24-26	27-29	30-32	33-35	36-38
Award money 10,000s of yen	none	.05	.10	.20	.30	.40	.50	.60	.80	1.0	1.5	2.0	3.0

Creative Idea Evaluation Score Table

	C 0-4	B 5-7	A 8-9	10-11	12-14	15-17	18-20	21-23	24-26	27-29	30-32	33-35	36-38
Benefit A													
Cost reduction (10,000s of yen/month)	0	no benefit				<1.5	1.5	3	5.5	8	12	16	24
Personnel reduction (number of persons)		no benefit				1	2	3	4	5	6	7	8
Equipment investment reduction (10,000s of yen/month)	0	no benefit				<1.5	1.5	3	5.5	8	12	16	24
Labor-hour reduction (hours/month)		no benefit			1	10	30	50	70	100		130	160
Labor-hour/personnel reduction (hours/month)		no benefit			1	55	110 or more						
Benefit B													
Space saved (m²)	0	less than prescribed		100 exterior		50 interior	1	25 office	200 exterior		100 interior	2	50 office
Safety					safer than before				safety maintained without extra effort				
Hygiene (environmental conditions)		no efficiency			environment improved; operation became easier				improved to the extent that it is not unpleasant; operations that cause fatigue are eliminated				
Quality (excluding quantitative)					product quality maintained or improved				occurrence of defects eliminated				
Other					slightly significant benefit				fairly significant benefit				

	0	1		2	
	0	**1**	**2**	**3**	**4**
Adaptability	none	can be used within section		can be used extensively within division	
Creativity	none	good because hints from others were applied		applicable and feasible; quite creative	
Originality	none	good originality because of hints from others		significant observation of troublesome problems	
Effort	none	made efforts		worked hard to implement; made fairly strong efforts	

- **Work demerits** (percentage reduction for suggestions related to one's own job)
- **Demerits for line employees with technical ability**

Subject	• Suggestions made by foremen and group leaders • Suggestions made by general employees with technical ability related to improving their jobs • Joint suggestions made by general employees with technical ability and those mentioned above	• Suggestions made by foremen and group leaders related to improving their jobs • Joint suggestions made by foremen and group leaders together with general employees with technical ability, related to improving their jobs
%	10%	20%

+

Involving administrative and technical workers in implementation	
Involving administrative and technical workers in implementation	
Worker received advice	Worker received cooperation or assistance
10%	20%

Figure 1-5. *Creative Idea Suggestion Evaluation Score Criteria Table*

39-41	42-44	45-46	47-48	49-50	51-52	53-54	55-56	57-58	59-61	62-64	65-67	68-70	71-73	74-75
4.0	5.0	6.0	8.0	10.0	11.0	12.0	13.0	14.0	15.0	16.0	17.0	18.0	19.0	20.0
9	10	11	12	13	14	15	16	17	18	19	20			
28	35	42	50	58	67	76	86	96	109	121	150 or more			
			1						2					3 or more
9	10	11	12	13	14	15	16	17	18	19	20			
28	35	42	50	58	67	76	86	96	109	121	150 or more			
200	250	300 or more												

safety maintained mechanically (without human attention)

	3	4	5
	300 exterior / 150 interior / 75 office	400 exterior / 200 interior / 100 office	500 exterior / 250 interior / 125 office
Safety	careless accidents prevented	extra safety precautions taken to prevent trouble	safety maintained in any kind of situation
Environment	troublesome environment improved; unnatural posture eliminated	workplace environment made more pleasant; stressful operations that had to be done in half-shifts are eliminated	created a superb environment that did not exist before; environment was improved or operations eliminated to a degree surpassing ordinary standards
Quality	defects eliminated; checks no longer necessary	quality and reliability improved; inspection eliminated	product value increased; company image improved
Overall	benefit	significant benefit	extraordinary benefit

3	4	5
can be used for same type of processing both at own factory and at other factories (suppliers)	can be widely used throughout the whole company, including diverse types of processing	wide range of applicability, both for whole company and for suppliers
excellent idea and means of implementing it; rather creative (can be submitted as an implementable new suggestion)	excellent idea and means of implementing it; very creative (patent application possible)	excellent idea and means of implementing it; extraordinarily creative (patent application possible)
good observation of neglected daily problem	excellent idea for solving major problem left untouched for a long time	extraordinary idea for dealing with major problem noticed by no one else for a long time
worked hard for a long time to implement; made rather strong efforts	worked very hard and made very strong efforts to overcome all problems involving implementation	hard work and effort at an extraordinary level in overcoming adverse circumstances

Demerits for administrative and technical staff

Subject	Suggestion somewhat related to own job	Suggestion substantially related to own job	Suggestion almost entirely related to own job
%	20%	30-40%	50% or more

Figure 1-5. Cont.

that are evaluated as deserving cash awards of ¥20,000 ($150) or more are screened once more by the Creative Idea committee. The cash awards for suggestions that pass this screening range from ¥20,000 to ¥200,000 ($150 to $1500), depending on the evaluation. The amounts for cash awards are determined by the end of each month.

In this manner, suggestions are screened and cash awards determined. Among these suggestions, those that have merited cash awards ranging from ¥10,000 to ¥40,000 ($75 to $300) receive the Creative Idea committee chairman's prize. Those meriting awards ranging from ¥50,000 to ¥200,000 ($375 to $1500) receive the company president's prize. These are monthly prizes, and the winners are honored at an award ceremony. They receive their awards in the presence of such executives as the Creative Idea committee chairman, the plant directors, and other members of top management.

Why Managers Make Presentations
on Employee Suggestions

During the screening process, a presentation about the content of each superior suggestion is given for top management executives, but the person who gives this talk is not the person who submitted the suggestion. Rather, the explanation is presented by the manager of that person's section. If managers try to talk about the contents of suggestions made by their workers with only a superficial understanding, they will not be able to answer the barrage of questions from the upper management and will be embarrassed. It is therefore important that managers give public talks about suggestions only after they get a thorough grasp of the suggestion's content.

Why is it necessary for section managers to give public talks about the suggestions of their subordinates? The people responsible for organizing each workplace play a central role in promoting Creative Idea suggestion activities. They should be expected to have a better understanding of Creative Idea suggestion activities than anyone else at the workplace. Managers who do not understand the content of their subordinates' suggestions are really not qualified to be managers. The presentation requirement helps them increase and deepen their understanding of Creative Idea suggestion activities.

Annual Prizes

Besides these monthly prizes, there are also annual prizes. There are three classifications: workplace prizes, individual prizes, and family prizes. The workplace prize is for Creative Idea suggestion activities that improve the workplace during the course of a year, from January to December. Since these activities are aimed at making an excellent workplace (at the divisional level), two or three divisions are chosen as excellent workplaces with a high suggestion rate per person (cash award amounts of ¥6000 ($45) or more).

Individual prizes are also for a period of a year from January to December. During the year, cash awards amounting to an average of ¥1000 ($7.50) or more per suggestion are given. From those who satisfy the criteria of five or more suggestions meriting ¥3000 ($22.50) or more, a total of 300 people are chosen and arranged in the order of the total amount of award money they have acquired during the year. The gold prize is awarded to the top 40, 60 receive the silver, and 200 the bronze. Besides these, individual prizes also are given to people who have received gold, silver, or bronze prizes for three years in a row in recognition of their achievements.

The third category of prizes, the family prize, is given to the 40 recipients of the gold prize and to the families of those who have received prizes during a period of three consecutive years.

Still another award is based on a person's achievements every year from August through July. Those who receive

---

Toyota Creative Idea Suggestion

Name (print):   Yumi Toyama   **Employee No.:** 2418736
Position: Machine operator   **Job code:**   XB240

Topic: Improving the reception system for the Ochanomizu dormitory lodging facilities

Submitted: 3 / 88
Implemented: 4 / 4 / 88
Not Yet Implemented: _____

Current Situation:

1. Lodging reservations for the company's Ochanomizu dormitory is handled by the Labor Section of the Headquarters Personnel Division
2. Reservation channels are as follows: Labor Section (fax, tel.) → Tokyo Personnel Section (mail, tel.) → dormitory. The Tokyo Personnel Section is responsible for the administration of this dormitory, and sending reservations through two offices serves no function but "going through channels," wasting labor-hours.

Improvement Suggestion:

1. The Tokyo Personnel Section should be put in charge of the lodging reservations now handled by the Labor Section (this would eliminate overlapping labor-hours within the company.
2. This would mean new work for the Tokyo Personnel Section, but it would also mean a significant reduction in labor-hours.
   - Reservation ledgers should be changed
   - People taking reservations by telephone should clearly print the person's position and name.
   - A fax machine should be installed in the dormitory; this would reduce the number of hours required for communicating information at the dormitory, while at the same time eliminating communication errors.
   - All members of the second welfare subsection should be able to handle reservations.
3. The above mentioned improvement plan should be implemented and reservations work should be transferred out of the Labor Section from March 1.

Resulting Benefits:

1. Transferring this work resulted in a reduction of the labor-hours required for reservations from 1772 minutes per month (29 hours, 32 minutes) to 680 minutes per month (11.5 hours).
2. Responses to applicants could be handled more smoothly, with improved service.
3. Because there are now fewer managers who have to be contacted for confirmation when there are lodging cancellations, and so on, things can be done more quickly and surely.

Figure 1-6. A Simplified Rendition of the Toyota Suggestion Form

Status		Scoring			
Status			**Original**	**Sub-committee**	**Committee**
Implemented: ____					
Adapted: √	To be tested ____	Benefit A	____	____	____
Under Study ____	Not adopted ____	Benefit B	6	____	____
		Adaptability	0	____	____
Award		Creativity	2	____	____
0 ____ ¥ 500 ____ ¥ 1,000 ____		Originality	4	____	____
¥ 2,000 ____ ¥ 3,000 ____ ¥ 4,000 √		Effort	4	____	____
¥ 5,000 ____ ¥ 6,000 ____ ¥ 8,000 ____		Demerit	-1	____	____
¥ 10,000 ____ ¥ 15,000 ____ ¥ 20,000 ____		**Total**	15	____	____
¥ 30,000 or more ____				Stamp:	Stamp:
		Evaluator	____	____	____
From the Review Committee: Thank you for your suggestion. You have tried hard to reduce the number of labor-hours by changing the location of the work.		File No.: _____			

Note: The original single-page Japanese form includes large sections for coding various information for machine reading as well as various other administrative sections. We have streamlined this version to show more clearly how the scoring and award information is recorded. A reproduction of the original form in Japanese appears in the Appendix. This example pertains to Example 2 in Chapter 4. – Ed.

Figure 1-6. Cont.

Explanation of Scoring for Superior Creative Idea Suggestions

(attached to suggestions meriting awards of ¥ 4,000 or more)

_____ Committee
_____ Subcommittee

Suggestion Title _____

Benefits:

Benefit	Benefit (amount of money, number of personnel)	score	total	Benefit and evaluation	score	total	possible score	total score
Benefit A	cost reduction			Benefit B			A20	
	labor reduction						B20	

Adaptability: (When this score is 3 points or more, list the other locations where the idea is applicable.)

	possible score	total score
	5	

Creativity:

	possible score	total score
	10	

Originality:

	possible score	total score
	10	

Effort:

	possible score	total score
	10	

The form contains the following fields and labels:

Demerits:

	total/ month points	labor-hours/ month points	demerit points

Work demerit point percentage

(always use when the person making a suggestion has demerit points or when a person with demerit points is involved in the suggestion)

Demerit point percentage of employees with technical skill

[%] [%]

enter 0 when there is nothing,
10% or 20% when there is something

=

Administrative and technical employees

[%]

enter 10% or 20%
when there is something

=

Demerit point percentage total

[%]

total score [points]

total score × demerit point percentage
= work demerit points

× [%]

total points [points]

work demerit points [points]

Cash award increased rank

Benefit A [ ]
Benefit B [ ]

Cash award amount

Figure 1-7. Scoring Explanation Form for Superior Suggestions

evaluations of five points or more for innovation and creativity of a suggestion that was awarded ¥20,000 ($150) or more have their names submitted as candidates for the Prefectural Science and Technology Director's Prize. This is done every year, with the applications submitted to the Aichi Prefecture office at the end of September.

Those whose suggestions are awarded this prize, after passing the preliminary prefectural screening as well as the second-level screening at the science and technology prefectural office, receive a special prize from the company, awarded on November 3, the anniversary of the founding of Toyota.

Using Award Money to Build Human Relations in the Workplace

At each plant in Toyota City, employees who made extraordinary increases in performance through Creative Idea suggestion activities were asked how prize money should be used. Kenji Homma, of the maintenance section in the main plant general assembly division, said that he did not have the extra time to make suggestions and that Creative Idea suggestion activities were completely left up to the direction of his subordinates. In spite of that, he received a silver prize in 1985. Asked about how the prize money that he had acquired should be used, Homma said, "Using it for myself is entirely out of the question. All prize money is used to strengthen ties of friendship among our colleagues at the workplace."

Masaru Kuwako, of the 22nd machining section in the Miyoshi plant second production division, has an extraordinary performance track record. He received bronze prizes in 1981, 1982, and 1987. He also received a gold prize in 1983, while receiving the three consecutive years prize in the same year, earning a reputation as a very hard worker. To improve the content of his job even more, Kuwako has been taking various national examinations and qualifying in some of them. Kuwako beamed with pride as he said, "I use most of the prize money I have received on myself."

But even though he claims to use the money for himself, by no means does he squander it. Rather, he uses the prize money to buy books he wants to read, or to buy reference materials he needs for passing national examinations. Kuwako continued, "What is left of my prize money after that, I use to contribute to dinner expenses for my colleagues who are working overtime to come up with creative ideas at the workplace."

Toshimitsu Matsunari, of the 13th machining section in the first machining division at the Kamigo plant, has a history of receiving prizes equal to that of Kuwako. He received gold prizes in 1985 and 1986. In 1987 he received a bronze prize as well as a three consecutive years prize. Matsunari is a forthright person whose candor can be seen in the statement, "I use one-third of my prize money for my own personal pleasure. The other two-thirds I spend on having a good time with my friends during the holiday celebrations at the workplace. That's because these events always improve human relations at the workplace."

Homma, Kuwako, and Matsunari are veteran employees. Since they have been working in positions giving them perspectives from which to consider the entire situation of several workplaces, perhaps it is only natural that their ideas about how to use prize money should be so strongly affected by their concerns for the workplace. Younger employees are in a different situation and one might suppose that many of them would spend all their prize money on themselves and their leisure time.

Although Shoji Nomura, of the machine maintenance section at the Motomachi plant, is young, he has a history of receiving prizes equal to those of the veterans. He received a bronze prize in 1985, a silver prize in 1986, and a gold prize in 1987. Besides receiving a three consecutive years prize in 1987, he also received a Prefectural Science and Technology Director's Prize. Nomura surprisingly gave an answer similar to those given by the veteran employees: "I use my prize money to get people together so that human relations at the workplace will be improved."

When Takaaki Shimamura, of the machining division maintenance section at the main plant, heard this, he replied with conviction, "If I take the attitude that I can use the prize money just for myself because I'm the one who received it, it will be hard for me to get cooperation from my colleagues the next time I try to come up with a creative idea. If that's the case, I won't be able to come up with a good suggestion, and I won't be able to receive prize money." Shimamura is younger than Nomura, but he was one of those whose excellent suggestion merited a Prefectural Science and Technology Director's Prize in 1985.

Haneda and Bando of the Creative Idea committee secretariat summed things up as follows:

> *The similarity of these answers might seem like pieces of candy that all look identical, but these people were not at all pressured into answering this way. No matter how many other employees you ask, they would all answer the same way. The point is, Creative Idea suggestion activities will not be successful unless there are good solid human relations among employees at the workplace. The employees who actually participate in these activities have an innate understanding of that fact. That is why all of them make progress and use their prize money to improve human relations at the workplace.*

On-site Actual Checks Contribute to a Suggestion Implementation Rate of More Than 90 Percent

In 1988, the total number of suggestions made by Toyota employees involved in Creative Idea suggestion activities surpassed 20 million, and more than 90 percent of these were actually used. Compared with other companies, this implementation rate would appear to be quite high.

A probing of why the implementation rate is so high suggests that the Toyota Creative Idea suggestion activities have unique features. Before the content of the proposed suggestions is evaluated by the subcommittee (the preliminary screening committee), the actual situation at each workplace is checked out by the workplace managers to find out whether the suggestion is feasible. This idea of "on-site actual checks" is a traditional way of thinking at Toyota.

This step in the screening goes beyond thinking while sitting at one's desk about whether some idea is feasible. Before thinking abstractly about whether something would be good or bad for selling some item, one first goes to where the customers are. Before considering whether the content of a suggestion will come through screening successfully, it should be actually checked out. Then, if it is feasible, the suggestion should be submitted. This is the main reason why the implementation rate has been increased.

The role of the workplace organizational structure is therefore important. The managerial role in Creative Idea suggestion activities lies in stimulating and supporting workplace suggestion activities, not just having people make suggestions. Whether suggestion activities become vigorous depends on whether employees are autonomously involved in suggestion activities. Workplace managers must create a supportive environment that makes it possible for employees to participate in suggestion activities.

Superiors and Subordinates Are
All in the Same Boat

A certain employee *M*, working for an office automation equipment manufacturer that has introduced a suggestion system, has had some unpleasant experiences in suggestion activities. *M*, who joined the company eight years ago, was interested in the suggestion system when it was explained to him around the time he first became an employee. Eager to make a good suggestion, he thought long and hard, eventually coming up with one, and submitted it. But it was not used. As he put it, "They said the suggestion I made after staying up all night for so many nights was no good. I was shocked by that." However, thinking that he should perhaps not expect a suggestion from a newcomer like himself to be adopted so easily, he pulled himself together and decided to make another suggestion.

Since his previous suggestion had not been adopted, this time he decided to first get his managers to look it over. If they said it was good, he would submit it just the way it was. But if they said there was some problem with it, he would consult them about it and reconsider the content of the suggestion.

But things did not turn out that way. *M*'s managers, shortly after considering his suggestion, severely criticized it, saying "This suggestion is so narrowly focused that it cannot be used." *M* was far more shocked than the previous time when he was informed that his suggestion could not be adopted. Since then, *M* has completely lost interest in suggestion activities. In his words, "The role of suggestions at work in our company is to meet suggestion quotas, so the managers put excessive pressure on us to make suggestions. We do not have any choice but to make them, but the way we really feel about it is that we have to force ourselves to perform an unpleasant task. No one should expect, therefore, that the suggestions we make will be good ones. And yet, because we have lost interest, we don't have any sense of shock even when our suggestions are not adopted."

Employees without much experience in suggestion activities are shocked when their suggestions are not adopted. This is likely to be the reason they shy away from suggestion activities. To avoid that kind of situation, Toyota's supervisors and managers conduct actual on-site checks of suggestions before they are submitted. The ones judged to be feasible are then submitted and screened by the subcommittee. Stimulating suggestion activities is another objective of actual on-site checks.

However, when employees submit suggestions to their managers for an actual on-site check, any effort to stimulate suggestion activities will be a complete waste of time if the employees are confronted with attitudes such as those of M's supervisors. Managers should be constantly paying careful attention to how they respond to employees who make suggestions, and Toyota has even drawn up a list of "tabooed" words not to be used by managers (see Figure 1-8).

This list reminds supervisors that they should not have a condescending attitude in leading the front-line employees who are their subordinates. Rather, their attitude should be one of willingness to think things out with these employees, showing an awareness that supervisors and workers are all in the same boat. Supervisors should not pressure those working for them to make suggestions. Without exaggeration, the most important mission of suggestion activities is for managers to build mutual relationships of trust with those who make suggestions.

Toshimi Onishi, the vice-chairman of the Creative Idea committee, emphasized that one of the factors contributing to the implanting of a Creative Idea Suggestion System is how managers react to suggestions from employees:

☐ Everyone understands *that!*
☐ We've never done that before, there's no point in trying it.
☐ I tried to do that before, and I know it won't work.
☐ This isn't up-to-date enough.
☐ Is this within the budget?
☐ There are just too many plans being made – I'll take a look at your opinion when I have time.
☐ Let's talk about this some other time.
☐ Let's wait a while and see how things turn out.
☐ Why do you want to change? Aren't things going okay now?
☐ There is a rule on this, so it's no good doing it that way.
☐ I don't think that's technically feasible.
☐ This idea is really off the wall, the manager will never agree to it.
☐ That's just not done at this company!
☐ That might work somewhere else, but certainly not here!
☐ The real world is more complicated than that.
☐ You don't really understand the situation, do you?
☐ Your suggestion is good, but the company can't afford it.
☐ This will create problems later on.
☐ Even if I give you advice, there's still no way.
☐ What *is* this suggestion? Can't you make it a little better?

Figure 1-8. Twenty Expressions to Avoid

Some companies manage their suggestion systems by having the managers in charge treat failures to meet quotas as so many points lost on test scores. But this is not the right way to deal with suggestion activities. Suggestion activities will not grow if management tries to dictate how ideas are suggested. At our company, people in management speak clearly about suggestions and in fact bend over backwards to see their good points so that suggestion activities become more vigorous.

Helping Employees Communicate Their Ideas

Making on-site checks at the workplace before screening suggestion content increases the suggestion adoption rate. In addition to having suggestions that they worked so hard to produce adopted, people want to earn a slightly higher evaluation and win a larger award. Getting a higher evaluation from the screening committee can depend on whether examples are entered on suggestion forms in a way that is easy to understand.

In the words of employee *K*, who works at the Kamigo factory, "Since my childhood, I have always had poor penmanship, and it required tremendous effort just to write sentences. So there was nothing I hated more than being told to write down my creative ideas. If possible, I want to avoid doing that." *K* has never submitted a suggestion during the six years since he entered the company. There seem to be quite a few cases like his.

As far as those who screen suggestions are concerned, since they read and evaluate more than two million suggestions a year while doing their regular jobs, not much time can be spent screening each suggestion. One member of a screening committee said: "Even if suggestions are at the same level, I give higher evaluations to those in which material about problem points, improvement points, and benefits is written so that it is easy to understand." There is nothing more troublesome for screening committee members than dealing with suggestions in which points are not clearly expressed. No matter how favorable an evaluation screening committee members might want to make, they cannot judge a suggestion to be really valuable when it lacks clarity.

An important role of supervisors, therefore, is to give advice about writing suggestions to those employees like *K*, whose penmanship is bad or who have trouble writing sentences. The first tip for people who do not write well is to tell them to put themselves in the position of the screening committee members who have to read what they write. Workers should try to spell words correctly, writing neatly and boldly. They should also be given concrete assistance to help them with sentence expression. This advice is also effective for employees who have little experience in suggestion activities.   The power to express suggestions well goes beyond just making correct sentences, however. It also includes other significant factors such as the extent to which suggestions are understood by those who make them and the depth of understanding in regard to the significance of a suggestion in relation to all the activities at a workplace. In short, skillful suggestion writing involves the ability to have perfect control in such matters. What is the problem? What kind of improvements should be made in dealing with it? What sort of efficiency will result from this? If these things are clearly understood, then they can be expressed in clear sentences.

The following four points of concrete advice are based on these ideas:

- When expressing things such as the current situation, the improvement proposal, the benefits, and so on, itemize in list form whenever possible. If the sentences are loosely connected, the point will be hard to grasp.
- Points within a suggestion that the author wants to emphasize the most should be underlined or written in bold with a felt-tipped pen to get the attention of screening committee members.
- If the suggestion writer has some doubts while writing, he or she should study the situation again and then write. If this seems like "too much trouble" and things are just left the way they are, the screening committee members and the writer both will be put in a difficult situation later.

- Even if something seems like just a small improvement, there may be considerable latent benefits that are not immediately obvious. It is important to organize ideas as efficiently as possible so that these become apparent.

Furthermore, those who find it difficult to write sentences should be advised to use drawings for those things they find especially difficult to put into writing. The term "drawing" does not mean something prepared according to strict specifications – a simple sketch is okay. Using drawings to express things is very effective. Expressing things in sentences can take hundreds of words, but the same thing can be expressed with just one drawing. Even screening committee members who do not have detailed knowledge of the workplace can clearly imagine the situation when a drawing is appended. This is helpful when they make evaluations.

Photographs or blueprints are also effective, but it is problematic to have these developed and printed outside the company. It is less desirable to use these as explanatory material for suggestions.

When various numerical values are involved – for example in comparing the situations before and after improvement – the use of tables will make things easier to understand. Even for suggestions regarding administrative work, efforts should be made to indicate numerical values whenever possible.

Employee *K*'s boss told him: "Your suggestion is hard to understand since your writing is not good; how about drawing pictures instead?" *K* did so, and received a ¥5000 ($40) cash award for his suggestion about improving tool-setting machine shop tools.

The Importance of Appropriate Guidance for the Development of the Individual Employee

With this kind of careful consideration, efforts are made so that employees become independently involved with

Creative Idea suggestion activities. But that does not mean that they can then be left on their own. Of course there are some employees who will grow naturally even if left on their own. There are also some employees, however, who become independently involved in suggestion activities, but do not get beyond the level of suggestion activity beginners. Managers are responsible for giving various kinds of advice to such employees.

There are several stages in Creative Idea suggestion activities, so guidance methods must be changed in accordance with these stages. Guidance for beginners focuses on small improvements to be made in the immediate vicinity of where they work, but those who make suggestions will be bored if they can only make small improvements, and this is likely to impede their growth. It is absolutely necessary to provide guidance that helps employees to accept the challenge of making improvements beyond the level of just accumulating small improvements.

Supervisor C said the following about his experience in giving this kind of advice:

> *When you have people fill out suggestion forms for proposing improvements, first make sure that those making suggestions are writing down exactly what they think. While writing down their own ideas, they all develop a basic grasp of things in the workplace, even when they haven't been thoroughly taught how to fill out the form. When there is a consensus that they should advance to the second stage at this point, they are first taught more advanced ways of doing things. This judgment is made after considering the suggestion content. It is made on the basis of whether or not the ideas involved differ from the ones submitted so far. When this stage begins is determined by good and bad evaluation materials affecting the guidance of each person. As long as*

there doesn't seem to be any new idea, guidance is repeated at the beginner's level. In any case, when the person who is guiding does not make progress and perform well, I feel that there will be no increased efficiency among the subordinates who are being guided.

As a means of guiding the development of Toyota employees who have gone beyond the beginners' level and have entered the second stage of making suggestions, they are asked to study specific subjects and to cope with problems of making improvements in groups. They learn to accept the challenges involved in making suggestions that will receive high evaluations. The following four points summarize the basic ideas involved in guiding people in this second stage:

- If people are making suggestions autonomously, it is sufficient just to give hints. If the persons doing the guiding force their opinions on subordinates, they will hinder the creative ideas of those who make suggestions.
- After a suggestion has been submitted, it does not end at that point. Views can be modified further; supervisors should help employees think about the situation from a broader perspective. This results in a gradual deepening of their understanding of improvements.
- As much as possible, employees are given external stimulation such as recommended reading, participation in training sessions, or the challenge of new work. They learn that there is a bigger world around them and although they have to travel further to reach their objectives, they will be rescued from dull routine.
- Employees are asked to set goals for themselves beyond those of the workplace and the company and then to accept the challenges this involves. Those in

leadership positions work as hard as they can to provide assistance such as the information, advice, and guidance needed by those who make suggestions.

Some specific guidance methods are given in Figure 1-9.

Managers Should Stimulate Suggestion Activities

In reaching for the second-stage objectives just described, it becomes clear how important the role of management is for Creative Idea suggestion activities. With no exaggeration, whether employees are independently involved in suggestion activities depends on whether managers are doing what they should do to stimulate these activities.

Taiichi Ohno, the former vice-president of Toyota Motor Company, established and implemented the Toyota production system that is the driving force behind Toyota's high profits. Since this production system was fundamentally different from the one that had been used until then, there was strong opposition from veteran workers who had become used to the old ways of doing things. Creative Idea suggestions also made changes in the methods that had been used until then. If there was a suggestion to make fundamental changes to a method thought up by one's manager, it was sometimes perceived as insubordination. But if the boss reacted by saying, "Who do you think you are?" then suggestion activities would not make any progress.

To make Creative Idea suggestion activities fruitful, managers must be careful about this sort of thing, and this involves making tremendous efforts. Moreover, these activities are always "work" that is outside of one's regular job. There is absolutely no remuneration for participating in them. Managers, more than ordinary employees, have to come up with ways to make involvement in suggestion activities independent from the requirements of the work.

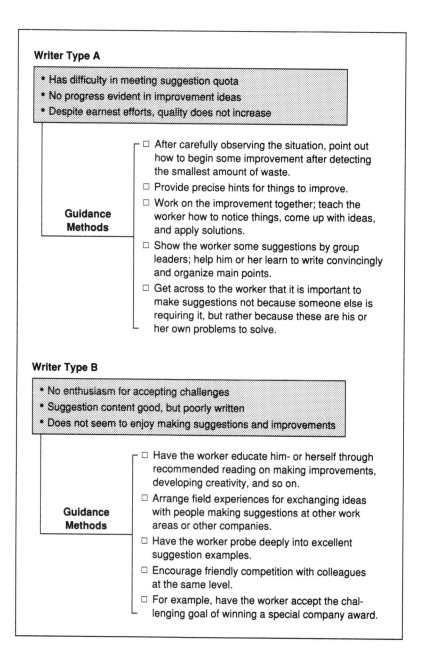

Writer Type A

* Has difficulty in meeting suggestion quota
* No progress evident in improvement ideas
* Despite earnest efforts, quality does not increase

Guidance Methods

☐ After carefully observing the situation, point out how to begin some improvement after detecting the smallest amount of waste.

☐ Provide precise hints for things to improve.

☐ Work on the improvement together; teach the worker how to notice things, come up with ideas, and apply solutions.

☐ Show the worker some suggestions by group leaders; help him or her learn to write convincingly and organize main points.

☐ Get across to the worker that it is important to make suggestions not because someone else is requiring it, but rather because these are his or her own problems to solve.

Writer Type B

* No enthusiasm for accepting challenges
* Suggestion content good, but poorly written
* Does not seem to enjoy making suggestions and improvements

Guidance Methods

☐ Have the worker educate him- or herself through recommended reading on making improvements, developing creativity, and so on.

☐ Arrange field experiences for exchanging ideas with people making suggestions at other work areas or other companies.

☐ Have the worker probe deeply into excellent suggestion examples.

☐ Encourage friendly competition with colleagues at the same level.

☐ For example, have the worker accept the challenging goal of winning a special company award.

Figure 1-9. How to Guide Second-stage Suggestion Writers

The Relationship Between Creative Idea Suggestion Activities and QC Circle Activities

At Toyota, there is vigorous participation in QC circle activities as well as in Creative Idea suggestion activities. Statistical Quality Control (SQC) was introduced in 1950, mainly in the inspection division. Total Quality Control (TQC), also known as company-wide quality control, was introduced in 1961. In 1964 a QC circle was formed at the subsection level, and in the following year it received the Deming Prize for performance. From 1966, TQC was expanded throughout the entire company. In 1975, autonomous QC circle activities began, and in 1980 Shoichiro Toyoda, the vice-president of the company (currently president), received the main Deming Prize.

Creative Idea suggestion activities and QC circle activities have similar characteristics as autonomous improvement activities. Moreover, both kinds of activities have similar objectives. It is very hard to distinguish clearly between these two kinds of activities because QC circles do not involve just quality control, but rather comprehensive improvement activities. And Creative Idea suggestion activities involve hands-on activity all the way from detecting problems to the eventual implementation of improvements.

As previously mentioned, those who make suggestions check out their idea at the workplace once before the suggestion is screened. But those who make suggestions should not rely only on their own judgment in testing suggestion content because when improvements are carelessly added to stable systems, it is possible to cause unanticipated inconvenience to workers involved at the same workplace or in other processes. In order to prevent unforeseen situations, it is absolutely necessary to get approval before implementing suggestion content. Furthermore, it is necessary to enlist the cooperation of colleagues and relevant staff members beforehand.

Those who make suggestions work as individuals from the time problem points are detected until the time the suggestion content is organized. But during the improvement implementation stage, studies are made with others, and various adjustments are made. This means going from doing things as an individual to doing things as a member of a team. This is probably one of the reasons why it is sometimes difficult to differentiate suggestion activities from QC circle activities, which are by nature small group activities.

From the perspective of employees engaged in Creative Idea suggestion activities or in QC circle activities, both kinds of activities are autonomous improvement activities that would seem to be distinguishable from each other only in terms of such differences as activity units, topic divisions, or ways of expressing results. For example, in QC circle activities there are units of six or seven persons per circle. The members comprising the group pursue a common topic during a fixed period of time. They search out the problem points involved and consider ways of solving them. They move closer toward their objectives by repeating implementation cycles. This process consists of accumulating improvements either from individual QC circle members or from several members working together.

In that sense, Creative Idea suggestion activities consist of organized small group activities such as QC circle activities. But they are not limited only to the quality-related topics adopted in QC circle activities. Topics can involve all kinds of irrationality, waste, and inconsistency at the workplace. QC circles select a topic that is suitable for circle activities from among the countless problems involved. They then try hard to come up with solutions in an organized way. QC circle activities adopt various aspects of Creative Idea suggestion activities and carry out small group improvement activities for those topics.

33496

Creative Idea suggestion activities at Toyota began in 1951. They were the foundation on which QC circle activities were established, beginning in the mid-1960s. Independent quality control study groups did not require so much time. Their metamorphosis into QC circle-type autonomous improvement circles seems to have occurred after suggestion activities had taken root at the workplace. As a result of QC circle activities struggling to make improvements in an organized manner at the small group level, Creative Idea suggestion activities became deeper and wider. Various improvement techniques brought about by QC circle activities spurred suggestion activities to probe into problem points more deeply. Another good influence of QC circle activity was their scientific and rational vantage point for considering how to cope with workplace problems.

Creative Idea suggestion activities, which invite the individual to act independently, grew more broadly and deeply as a result of being influenced by organized improvement activities such as those of QC circles. Improvements that could not be handled by QC circles were entrusted to the suggestion process.

These two kinds of independent improvement activities, involving Creative Idea suggestion activities and QC circle activities, reinforced each other while increasing each other's efficiency. These activities are linked like two wheels on a bicycle.

Suggestion Activities of Toyota Workers Overseas

In April 1989, Toyota made a formal announcement that it would construct an assembly plant in the Midlands of England. If things go according to plan, this plant will be completed in 1992, the same year that the European Community market will be integrated. Even in Toyota's overseas production plants, the Creative Idea Suggestion System is gradually being introduced.*

Masami Watanabe, employed in the first body section of the vehicle body division at the Motomachi factory, worked hard to introduce a Creative Idea Suggestion System at the production site as a resident employee of Toyota-Mobilindo in Indonesia (absorbed into Toyota Astra Automobiles, Ltd. in January 1989). Shortly after Watanabe was sent to Mobilindo, Kyokazu Kodama (of the press section in the main factory vehicle body division) who had begun suggestion and QC circle activities there, proceeded to a new appointment, so Watanabe immediately inherited responsibility for these. (These events are described further in Chapter 3).

Watanabe explained the Creative Idea Suggestion System completely but simply to the employees at the Mobilindo workplace. But when he tried to implement it, workers did not make suggestions as he thought they would. As he put it, "I was just not able to get them to understand the meaning of improvement. I wondered how I should explain this. As I focused all my attention, working alone day and night in a foreign country, I just got more and more irritated."

Watanabe was a member of the GI (Good Idea) Club, an autonomous activities circle, one of the Creative Idea suggestion activities (see Chapter 3). (After returning to Japan he served as its president.) Watanabe decided to consult with his colleagues in the GI Club about the difficult position he was in. At the same time, he thought about getting advice from the Creative Idea committee secretariat about how to stimulate Creative Idea suggestion activities.

---

* The suggestion system is also an integral element of Toyota's ventures in the United States, active at the Georgetown, Kentucky facility of Toyota Motor Manufacturing, Inc., and also at New United Motor Manufacturing, Inc. (NUMMI), a joint venture between Toyota and General Motors. – Ed.

How should this system be established? Every day there are more and more problems. After sending facsimile copies about these problems to the GI Club and to the Creative Idea committee secretariat, I received their responses. Using them as reference material, I guided my employees gently but firmly, making it easy for them to understand how we could solve problems. This gradually resulted in the emergence of genuine Creative Idea suggestion activities at the workplace. By the time I returned to Japan, sheets of paper with the word kaizen (continuous improvement) written on them were displayed everywhere in the Indonesian plant.

The efforts begun by Kodama and Watanabe are now being repeated at other overseas offices and plants. The Creative Idea committee secretariat has produced an English-language pamphlet entitled *The Creative Idea Suggestion System* to make the system easy to understand for people working in overseas offices and plants.

Tsuyoshi Bando of the Creative Idea committee secretariat adds the following:

As the secretariat, we should rightfully take the initiative in giving advice to those engaged in overseas suggestion activities, but at present we are not doing so. When people consult us, as Mr. Watanabe did, we cooperate with them. But Toyota has many overseas plants. And when consideration is given to a situation in which Creative Idea suggestion activities are gradually emerging at those plants, I think the time has come when we must seriously consider how we, as the secretariat, should be involved with them. This will definitely continue to be a big problem for the secretariat.

According to Toshimi Onishi, the vice-chairman of the Creative Idea committee, the total amount of award money for Creative Idea suggestions comes to between ¥1.4 billion and ¥1.5 billion ($10.7 million to $11.5 million). This is because there are two million suggestions per year and it is assumed that the average amount of award money per suggestion ranges from ¥700 to ¥800 ($5 to $6). As Onishi put it:

> *Although the economic benefit that derives from suggestions cannot be calculated exactly, I suppose it is probably equivalent to about ten times the total amount of award money, which would mean around ¥15 billion ($115 million). Toyota sales amount to about ¥7 trillion ($53.8 billion) and its production costs are about ¥4 trillion ($30.7 billion). Assuming that the production cost for in-house work ranges from ¥1 trillion to ¥1.5 trillion ($7.7 billion to $11.55 billion), the ¥15 billion of economic benefit generated by Creative Idea suggestions is equivalent to about 1 percent of these internal manufacturing costs.*

This means that Creative Idea suggestion activities have enormous economic efficiency. An editorial in a special edition of the *Toyota Creative Idea News* (Sept. 13, 1951), entitled "From Routine Job Performance to Creative Ideas," appeared at the time when Toyota made its first appeal for suggestions after introducing the Creative Idea Suggestion System. It noted:

> *This system is not at all new. It has been implemented in all parts of our country since ancient times. But the reason why it has failed to bear excellent fruit is that there were probably problems of management and organization. . . . It can be assumed that the democratization of management itself is essential for the ideas of employees to be broadly disseminated among managers. . . . Whether these Creative Idea suggestion activities will really flourish depends of course on the company, but it also depends on the constant efforts that we make in the future.*

Japan's independence has finally become imminent. This obviously means that economically a balance has been achieved between the country's revenue and expenditures. And it means that Japan has exported as much as possible. It is important to reduce costs in order to export. The cars that we make must be sufficiently competitive not only with cars in the domestic market, but also with foreign cars in foreign markets. Our supreme mission, therefore, is to aim constantly at the improvement of our vehicles while at the same time lowering costs as far as possible. . . . If our intention is at least to earn our livelihood by making cars, then how can we let ourselves become constantly infatuated with playing mah-jongg or pachinko?

It is no exaggeration to state that during the years since this statement, Toyota's Creative Idea suggestion activities, together with its production system and waste reduction activities, have become the driving force that produces the company's high profits.

CHAPTER TWO

The Formation of the Creative Idea Suggestion System

What Toyota Learned from Ford Motor Company

The Creative Idea Suggestion System at Toyota Motor Company was born in 1951. The previous year on July 11, 1950, Eiji Toyoda, a director at the time (promoted to managing director, July 18, 1950), and now president, went to the United States and stayed about three months to observe the automobile situation in the United States, the world's leading nation in the automobile industry. Eiji stayed during that time at the River Rouge plant of the Ford Motor Company in Detroit and observed Ford production facilities and manufacturing techniques.

Back in Japan, Eiji talked about his impressions:

> There at the largest Ford plant, there was a feeling of pride, as might be expected. I was amazed at the gigantic scale of facilities, organization, and everything else. First, the area of the building, 15 million square feet, made the Ford plant nearly ten times the size of the Toyota Koromo plant. Inside the building there were blast furnaces and glass factories, docks, machine shops, assembly lines, and cupolas, which were operated according to a policy of self-support and

self-sufficiency in one integrated process to produce automobiles. Ford employees numbered 70,000, and perhaps because there were two or three production shifts due to the influence of the recent Korean War, production had risen to a rate of 7000 vehicles per day. Of these, 700 vehicles, or about ten percent, were assembled at the River Rouge plant, while parts for assembly were sent to Ford assembly plants in various parts of the United States to assemble the other 90 percent.

But just how is mass production done? As I mentioned before, the River Rouge plant is the largest of the Ford Motor Company, but size alone does not ensure flawless automobile production. Even though we say that there was still some room for improvement in our production organization, what caught our attention most of all was material handling (transport management). Ford used a particularly advanced conveyor for material handling. The conveyor wound around through the plant, extending 120 miles in serpentine fashion. This meant all the various types of raw materials and parts were totally linked together, and while the vehicle was gradually being completed, everything would be merged and combined into one final assembly line without any mistakes.*

At that time Japan's automobile industry was at the dawn of a new era. Toyoda's remarks simply express his amazement at the time when he went on his own from Japan, about to become an advanced automobile producing nation, and confronted the gigantic scale of the American automobile industry.

Toyoda is said to have predicted at the time that Japan would also become a motorized society in the near future.

---

* This quotation is from *Toyota: A 30 Year Commemorative History*, published in Japanese. – Ed.

Eiji Toyoda, current chairman of the Creative Idea Suggestion Committee

The sight of the enormous conveyor system in Ford's River Rouge plant aroused a fierce, combative spirit in him. There can be no doubt that he hoped to overtake Ford someday.

On October 3 as Toyoda's stay in the United States was coming to an end, the late Shoichi Saito, a Toyota Motor Company director who later served as chairman, left Japan to come to the United States. His mission was to stay approximately six weeks at the same Ford plant to study production facilities and factory management methods. After this, he was to visit other places, such as processing machinery manufacturers, parts manufacturers, American automotive engineering societies, and American automobile industrial organizations. He returned to Japan on January 31, 1951.

On returning, Saito published his research findings in a book entitled *America, the Automobile Nation*, published in Japan in September, 1952. Written in the first decade of the postwar era, this book is precious material, describing in detail the actual state of the American automobile industry, with

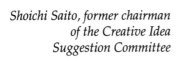

Shoichi Saito, former chairman of the Creative Idea Suggestion Committee

Ford at the heart of it. Saito discusses in this book the production technology of the American automobile industry:

First of all, the problem of production volume is the underlying premise for production technology in the automotive industry. Various parts are produced at a rate of about 6000 per day, and consequently the manufacturing machinery is simplified and automated. In addition, advanced material handling methods, which combine this machinery in organic fashion, increase the efficiency of the facilities to a high degree. All of this naturally lowers costs.

The grand scale of production is even more fascinating than production technology advances. Accordingly, from a production volume perspective, if one looks at the Japanese automotive industry and facilities and at companies of the same level, it is correct to say there is no great disparity. However, while one cannot ignore thinking about production volume altogether, in terms of production technology, the difference becomes clear with the constant zealous advances in speeding up the cutting process, toward application over a wide spectrum at a high frequency, conversion of forging technology, and so on.

As a result of Saito's study, a "Five-year Plan for Production Facility Modernization" was established. By implementing this plan, manufacturing technology was significantly improved and material handling methods advanced considerably. Toyota's production facilities were substantially rationalized.

The Ford Suggestion System

When Toyoda and Saito visited the River Rouge plant, they took notice of Ford's suggestion system. In this system, suggestions were not confined to technical or manufacturing improvements, and any employee could present an idea on his or her own initiative, however trivial it might be.

At the time the system was established, Henry Ford II talked about it in the following way, seeking to gain the employees' understanding and cooperation:

> *In any organization that becomes as large as Ford, a mutual exchange of ideas gets to be very difficult. On this occasion, therefore, we have established a suggestion system. In this system, you ladies and gentlemen submit your original ideas one after another on how to improve work and upgrade working conditions, and we will try them out at a special location. Those suggestions that obtain good results will be implemented on a company-wide basis. I have no doubts that the great majority of you have excellent suggestions on how to do things better, simpler, and more safely in order to increase production. However, these suggestions have yet to be proposed and implemented. This company of ours needs your original ideas. As to just how to make your work the best, there is no one with better knowledge than you. To those of*

you whose suggestions are adopted and implemented from among those submitted, we will present a sizable cash prize, and give ample recognition for such cooperation. This suggestion system gives you the opportunity to make known your creative ideas. The suggestions will be considered fairly and without delay by a committee of experts. And we are committed to awarding appropriate prizes to those of you whose suggestions are adopted.*

At Ford, suggestions were defined in the following way: "Suggestions are constructive concepts. That is, they are more practical or safer methods; they improve work or procedures. Or, to put it another way, they improve work, or they promote the welfare of the employees. In general, the most useful idea is the one applicable to one's own work." The entries in Figure 2-1 concretely illustrate good suggestions along with suggestions ineligible for awards in the Ford system.

Concerning who was qualified to submit suggestions, "all employees are eligible to receive awards excluding supervisors and those persons whose official duties are of a creative nature." The occupational categories that disqualified those people in them are also pointed out. However, employees in certain occupational categories, for example, factory workers and die-sinkers, foremen, experimenters, machine tool repairmen, maintenance personnel, and tool repairmen, could receive awards for those suggestions unrelated to their respective official duties.

To give guidance on how to develop original ideas, items such as those in Figure 2-2 were presented in concrete terms. "The greatest pleasure in human life is to do something even

---

* This is a translation of a quotation from the original *Ford Plant Handbook*, quoted by Saito in his book. The availability of the original English version is unknown. – Ed.

Examples of Good Suggestions	• Improving machine operations • Improving production methods • Improving handling materials • Improving external appearance of products • Improving quality • Improving working conditions • Preventing damage to tools • Reducing trash • Reducing work hours • Eliminating useless work • Eliminating trouble caused by red tape • Improving welfare of employees • Improving safety equipment
Examples of Suggestions Ineligible for Prizes	• Ideas already submitted by other employees • Ideas under consideration by the company • Ideas submitted by persons not allowed to make suggestions • Suggestions for doing routine work obvious to everyone • Suggestions related to purchase of parts or materials • Suggestions related to unfinished work in manufacturing, processing methods, and so on
Occupational Categories Disqualifying Persons from Making Suggestions	• Engineers • Operation standards personnel • Process technology personnel • Cost accounting personnel • Machine designers • Foremen

Figure 2-1. Basic Features of the Ford Suggestion System

Idea Points

Materials: Can't articles be substituted that are of higher quality and lower cost, and are easier to obtain? Can't scrap material be used more effectively?

Machinery: Are machines performing at maximum capacity for each operation? Is this the best machine for this work? Can't machines or workers be used that are available on-site?

Equipment and tools: Is it possible to use the most appropriate equipment, tools, fixtures, and jigs (tools used for holding the processed material with precision against the cutting edges of working machine tools)?

Machine layout: Is work flow retrogression kept at a minimum? Is manual transport kept at a minimum?

Production design: Do design changes make significant reductions in the amount of time and materials?

Safety: Are these methods the safest and simplest possible? Is the proper safety equipment ready for use?

Ideas
a. changing simple fixtures
b. chucks that operate quickly
c. removing items from jigs
d. improving maintenance methods

Solutions
a. jigs that are easy to handle
b. machines that allow faster installation
c. methods of easy removal
d. safe, reliable tools

Other
• development of new methods
• omitting unnecessary details
• combining of specifications or operations
• rearranging to increase good results
• simplifying all required specifications

Figure 2-2. Guidelines for Developing Original Ideas in the Ford Suggestion System

better than what was done before. Analyze your own work. Do all operations on the chart (handling materials, mechanical, and manual operations). Answer your own questions. Why is something necessary? Who is best qualified to do it? What is the objective? By when should it be finished? Where should it be implemented? What is the best method?"

The suggestions from all employees were entered on suggestion forms, and either put into the provided suggestion box or collected after being sent by mail. The suggestions submitted were checked to see if they qualified or not. The ones that did qualify were scrutinized by experienced members of the screening committee. The screening of complicated suggestions that were hard to examine sometimes took several weeks. After a thorough examination, the suggestion was discussed by members of the suggestion committee.

If the suggestion was adopted by the suggestion committee, the person who submitted it was informed, and a check was presented a few days later. On the other hand, when the suggestion was not adopted, it was returned to the person who made it, and a member of the screening committee met with him or her to explain why the suggestion was not adopted.

A suggestion not adopted could not be resubmitted until one year from the day it was rejected. After the year elapsed, a reevaluation was mandatory; the suggestion could be improved and submitted once again.

The prize money for adopted suggestions was determined in the following manner:

> For improvements where the economizing could be measured directly, a cash payment was made that was equivalent to 100 percent of the calculated savings per month in labor and materials multiplied by two months.
>
> For example, if your suggestion reduced construction and materials costs by $100 per month, the prize money was $100 multiplied by two months, or $200. The cost of implementing

the suggestion was not deducted from the prize money, and the amount saved in operating costs was not taken into account. In addition to considering the profit received from using a suggestion, the company made a decision about prize money from the perspective of other improvements involved.

When a suggestion was adopted, the minimum amount of prize money was $5 for a suggestion used by the company and the maximum amount was $1500. The company also awarded special prizes for suggestions of exceptional merit. Legal deductions such as income taxes were made at the time of the award. Company decisions on qualifications, adoptions, rejections, or prizes were final.

The Tradition of Respect for the Spirit of Creativity at Toyota

A suggestion system meant the budding of a management planning participation consciousness, raised work motivation, and increased management efficiency in a big way. For Eiji Toyoda and Shoichi Saito, these were things they cared about deeply.

Toyota has struggled to create a company atmosphere in which great importance is attached to creative spirit. From its beginning Toyota has based its principles on the last instructions of Sakichi Toyoda, the founder of Toyota Automatic Loom Works, who began the industrial enterprise of the Toyota group. The enterprise goals of the articles of incorporation, on his instruction, include an article entitled, "Invention Research and Its Application." Furthermore, the company preamble contains a declaration, "you should put yourself wholeheartedly into study and creation, and anticipate the trends of the day."

Kiichiro Toyoda, the founder of Toyota Motor Company, also attached great importance to the creative spirit and is said to have never criticized anyone so that creative zeal would not be crushed. He acted this way even when something ended in failure, so long as it happened while the individual involved was enthusiastically coping with the challenges of the job.

To institutionalize the value placed on creative spirit, which existed from the beginning, the following provisions were incorporated in the work regulations that were laid down on November 1, 1938:

> *People in the following categories, upon selection, shall receive a bonus, which shall be announced:*

1. People able to invent or improve machinery and tools related to work.
2. People able to develop ideas expected to promote work preparations or lead to good results due to them.
3. People able to invent methods related to economizing and utilization of materials and supplies.

The Creative Idea Suggestion System is based on this tradition of creative spirit. A modification of the Ford suggestion system adapted to Toyota was put into effect in May 1951, immediately after Toyoda and Saito returned from the United States. At the same time, the Creative Idea committee was established as the promotion and review organization of this system, with Saito serving as its first chairman. In June the first suggestions were collected, and on August 16, of the 183 entries, 21 received commendations as excellent suggestions.

In addition to the Creative Idea Suggestion System with total employee participation, an Invention and Idea System for technical experts was instituted at Toyota.

With the aim of further promoting the creative spirit, Toyota established invention and idea management regulations on February 1, 1949, to award grants to technicians and engineers who produced superior inventions and ideas related to business. The rights to these inventions belonged to the company; although it gained the patent rights, utility model rights, design rights, copyrights, and so on, the creators received compensation during the term of existence for those rights.

An invention and idea committee was established as the screening agency for these proposals, and the first committee began on March 4, 1949. Eiji Toyoda, who was a director and head of the technical department at the time, served as its first chairman.

In contrast with the Invention and Idea System, which is limited to technical experts, the Creative Idea Suggestion System is for all employees. In it, employees can make suggestions in an informal manner on anything, irrespective of their individual qualifications. Creative Idea suggestions that are appropriate are examined by the Invention and Idea committee, and applications for patent rights, utility model rights, and the like, are possible. The two systems maintain close, mutual connections, and by being integrated, perform their role of promoting the creative spirit.

The History of Suggestion Systems in Japan

Just as Toyota's Creative Idea Suggestion System was modeled after the Ford suggestion system, the suggestion system in Japan generally has American roots.

The first suggestion system in the United States was introduced by the Eastman Kodak Company in 1898. The first suggestion submitted proposed having the windows washed to improve lighting in the workplace. For this suggestion a prize of two dollars was awarded. As research into human relations advanced rapidly in the United States during the early twentieth century, an increasing number of enterprises introduced suggestion systems. Prior to World War II virtually all American enterprises had adopted the suggestion system.

This sort of activity promptly caught on in Japan, and Hitachi was the first in Japan to introduce the suggestion system in 1930. After that, Yasukawa Denki in 1932 and Origin Denki in 1938 adopted a suggestion system in which ideas for improvement were collected from the employees. However, in the prewar period these enterprises were about the only ones to introduce the suggestion system. According to a 1985 survey by the Japan Human Relations Association (JHRA) of 604 businesses about suggestion activities, only 1.4 percent of all the enterprises had introduced the suggestion system prior to 1949.

Toyota's Creative Idea Suggestion System started in 1951. According to the survey above, 7.1 percent of the 604 business enterprises adopted the suggestion system between 1950 and 1954.

Between 1955 and 1964, 31.9 percent of the 604 businesses adopted the suggestion system. One center of growth was the manufacturing sector, and in this period the suggestion system became more and more visible. QC circle activities were vigorous in the late 1950s, and there may be a link between this and the fact that companies adopting suggestion activities began to increase.

According to the same survey, 36.1 percent of the 604 businesses adopted the suggestion system between 1975 and 1984. This shows that at the time of the oil crises, although the Japanese economy entered a period of slow growth, the suggestion system expanded beyond its already flourishing position in the major manufacturing companies to reach more medium-sized companies. Moreover, retail and financial businesses and other service industries, which had previously not used the suggestion system, took an interest in it and began to adopt it. This probably also influenced the increased number of businesses that started the suggestion system during this period.

Valuing Improvement in Management over Economic Results

Hardship is a partner to any pioneering venture. The Japanese enterprises starting the suggestion systems around 1950 were the pioneers of Japan's suggestion system. Because Toyota's Creative Idea Suggestion System was introduced in 1951, it too was a trailblazer in Japan's suggestion activities.

When Toyota introduced the Creative Idea Suggestion System, the employees at first mistook creative ideas to mean things related to great inventions. For that reason in the first year (1951) there were 789 suggestions and awards totaling ¥343,000 ($2638). Both the quality and the quantity of the suggestions were rather low.

Eiji Toyoda and Shoichi Saito's objectives in introducing the Creative Idea Suggestion System at Toyota after their visits to the River Rouge Ford plant were to increase conscious participation in managing the work process through employee involvement, as well as to increase economic savings. The results for the first year, however, failed to reach their objectives on both counts.

Consequently, Saito, as committee chairman, began to emphasize quantity, and efforts were made to increase the number of suggestions. Creative ideas enable employees to improve their work and further their own welfare. The committee repeatedly explained that creative ideas could improve problem areas employees encountered every day and encouraged the employees to participate. In the beginning, the word "idea" in Creative Idea Suggestion System was written in *kanji* (formal characters), but to soften the stiff tone this conveyed, it was changed to the *hiragana* (phonetic) alphabet

Year	Number of Suggestions	Suggestions per Person	Participation Rate (%)	Adoption Rate (%)
1951	789	0.1	8	23
1952	627	0.1	6	23
1953	639	0.1	5	31
1954	927	0.2	6	53
1955	1,087	0.2	10	43
1956	1,798	0.4	13	44
1957	1,356	0.2	12	35
1958	2,682	0.5	18	36
1959	2,727	0.4	19	33
1960	5,001	0.6	20	36
1961	6,660	0.6	26	31
1962	7,145	0.6	20	30
1963	6,815	0.5	21	34
1964	8,689	0.5	18	29
1965	15,968	0.7	30	39
1966	17,811	0.7	38	46
1967	20,006	0.7	46	50
1968	29,753	0.9	43	59
1969	40,313	1.1	49	68
1970	49,414	1.3	54	72
1971	88,607	2.2	67	74
1972	168,458	4.1	69	75
1973	284,717	6.8	75	77
1974	398,091	9.1	78	78
1975	381,438	8.7	81	83
1976	463,442	10.6	83	83
1977	454,552	10.6	86	86
1978	527,718	12.2	89	88
1979	575,861	13.3	91	92
1980	859,039	19.2	92	93
1981	1,412,565	31.2	93	93
1982	1,905,642	38.8	94	95
1983	1,655,868	31.5	94	95
1984	2,149,744	40.2	95	96
1985	2,453,105	45.6	95	96
1986	2,648,710	47.7	95	96
1987	1,831,560			96
1988	1,903,858			96

Figure 2-3. Changes in the Number of Suggestions, Participation Rate, and Adoption Rate in Toyota Suggestion Activities

spelling. Making the employees feel that the system was not so formal was one more way to boost quantity.

Toyota has a tradition of valuing creative spirit. With such an atmosphere at the company, the Creative Idea Suggestion System became firmly established when it was introduced, and a "pioneer spirit" seized many employees. Affected by this traditional valuing of the creative spirit, the Creative Idea committee's efforts to boost quantity gradually bore fruit.

From 1965 onwards the number of suggestions grew by leaps and bounds. In 1974 the number finally reached 1 million. In 1979 it was 3 million, and by 1984 it had jumped to 10 million (see Figure 2-3).

In sharp contrast, the original Ford suggestion system, which served as the model for Toyota's Creative Idea Suggestion System, declined year by year and finally disappeared. Why did this happen? Tsuyoshi Bando, a member of the Toyota Creative Idea committee secretariat, explained the circumstances under which Ford ended its original suggestion system:

> American suggestion systems stress economic benefits. Ford also made this its highest priority when its suggestion system was in effect. As a result, the employees who made suggestions also thought only of their own "economic benefit." That is, they were not satisfied with the amount of prize money. Because the suggestions they submitted brought great economic benefits to the company, they wanted the company to increase the amount of prize money. When employees who submitted suggestions began to demand cash awards equal to half the actual value of the economic benefits gained, management lost all interest in continuing the suggestion system.

The results of a 1984 survey by the JHRA comparing Japanese and American suggestion systems clearly reveal that

U.S. suggestion systems in general and not just the original Ford suggestion system, place priority on economic efficiency. The survey showed the number of suggestions per person as 24 for Japan and 0.16 for the United States; the U.S. rate was 1/123 that of Japan's. And, for participation rate, for Japan it was 60 percent and for the United States it was 13 percent. Furthermore, the rate of suggestions adopted was 82 percent for Japan and 22 percent for the United States (see Figure 2-4).

On the other hand, in terms of economic benefits yielded per suggestion adopted, it was ¥13,034 ($100) for Japan and ¥724,208 ($5500) for the United States. Looking at the average award money paid for suggestions adopted, it was ¥570 per suggestion ($4.40) for Japan and ¥71,190 per suggestion ($550) for the United States. In the United States, the award therefore represented approximately 1/10 the economic savings resulting from the adoption of a suggestion.

The JHRA analyzed the results of the survey in the following way.

In the American suggestion system, the company buys the idea from the individual. The company evaluates whether the idea will yield a definite monetary value. In a word, it is result oriented.

In Japanese suggestion activities, employees make even very modest improvements in the work they are in charge of, continually creating in a quick and easy manner an environment where the work can be done with confidence. Each person who is in charge of a worksite also best knows the work and makes small improvements based on his or her familiarity with things. This situation is multiplied many times by all the individuals there. Because of this, employees have a problem consciousness and keep a close check on the tendency to carelessly overlook problems.

For any problem point discovered, they ask what can be done to make it better, learn methods for improvement, put them to practical application, receive advice from supervisors, consult with associates, and summarize this knowledge in suggestions. In this sort of process, it is very important not to limit evaluations to only those suggestions that simply improve efficiency. In many cases, even if no monetary savings can be found, a cash award is made for such perception and effort, and an evaluation is done.

The role of the Japanese suggestion system is not simply to produce efficiency along American lines. Its scope is much broader and includes raising management planning participa-

Japan	Items Compared	United States
24	Suggestions/ Person/Month	0.16
60%	Participation Rate	13%
82%	Adoption Rate for suggestions	22%
¥ 13,034 ($100)	Economic benefit produced per suggestion adopted	¥ 724,208 ($5,500)
¥ 570 ($4.40)	Amount awarded per suggestion adopted	¥ 71,190 ($550)

Japan Human Relations Association survey for 1984
(Values computed at ¥ 130/dollar and rounded.)

Figure 2-4. A Comparison of Japanese and American Suggestion Systems

tion consciousness through total employee participation, building thinking habits, developing creative idea abilities, and implementing the value of work through the joy of creating. Moreover, through the use of suggestions, the level of consciousness building, and the development of abilities can be continuously measured. The workplace is built up by all the employees, becoming a source of strength that supports the management of Japan.

Improvement in Management Begins with Awareness of Participation

It is clear that the Japanese suggestion system, which started with Toyota's Creative Idea Suggestion System, gave virtually all priority to improvement in management. What does this improvement mean in concrete terms?

The JHRA describes three phases in improvement in management through a suggestion system.

1. The strength of Japanese management is not to be found in large numbers of people increasing efficiency by working according to standards and manuals created by a few talented persons. Rather, it is in the massed strength of many individuals concentrating on their own duties, having problem consciousness, eliminating even slightly inconvenient aspects of the work before them, and making improvements to increase efficiency.

   Through suggestion activities, everyone has the chance once or twice a month to re-evaluate his or her own work. In addition, employees consider improvements for problems in small groups. They consult with supervisors and experienced employees, and also receive advice, becoming aware that everyone is linked together to improve the workplace.

2. Various means are adopted to develop employees' abilities. Concrete activities, such as individual guidance through evaluation of suggestions, mutual development within a group, or individual information gathering, bring a large measure of personal growth to the workplace. The problems that are taken up are real cases, and the processes whereby employees endeavor to find the solutions and make improvements are steadily accumulated as a visible broadening of individual experience and ability.

   Workers' acquired problem-solving abilities or abilities to make improvements will be manifested in daily activities (not necessarily in the form of a suggestion), raising the quality of work for individuals and teams, increasing work efficiency, and becoming a force that contributes to the company's bottom line results. It is likely that greater importance will be attached to individual growth through suggestions in the future.

3. By means of total employee participation and by raising the suggestion-making ability of each person, the resulting quality of suggestions and the substance of the improvements become better.

   In evaluating suggestions in Japan, the trend is toward assessing efficiency not only in monetary terms, but also in terms of more intangible benefits. This includes improvement of fundamental conditions that must not be neglected in Japanese business activities, such as safety, the company image, customer relations, and so on.

   Japanese suggestion activities do not consist solely of asking how much more cheaply something can be made or of reducing losses, but include the goal of improving the atmosphere and morale of the entire workplace or the entire company.

   Of course, when the person in the front line of activities who has the best understanding of the situation comes up with improvements that yield sizable economic benefits, the result is not just a plus for the company, but for the workers as well because the expansion in benefits also improves their lives.

Because "employment" in Japan is often a lifetime arrangement with one company, the quality of an employee's life is closely linked to that of the workplace. Even if the immediate rewards are small compared to the outcome, this results in efficiency in which everyone shares their knowledge to strengthen the workplace.

Based on the three points above, the JHRA came to the following conclusion about the benefits of improvement for management.

The Japanese suggestion system is multifaceted and functions in stages. It is therefore meaningless to say simply that these suggestion activities constitute a system. One should continually ask to what extent their content has been put into effect and whether they are linked to the goals of management activity.

The basis of all this is a leadership that supports suggestions, a secretariat staff for suggestions, and administrative supervisors who are pivotal in promoting suggestions. Through conscientious performance, these three elements establish a climate for suggestion activities throughout the organization and motivate the people who make suggestions.

If leadership, staff, or administrators regard suggestions as something extra or as things that someone else should promote, then they should recognize that activities will cease.

The first step is to ask employees to participate in suggestion activities, to increase the number of suggestions. By doing this, many employees will become involved in suggestion activities and through their own study or that of their fellow associates, they will personally experience the pleasure of creative ideas. At that point the quality of the suggestions will also improve.

The Toyota Suggestion System's Growth Period

Toyota's Creative Idea Suggestion System followed the development path just described, beginning with a focus on participation (quantity) and moving to higher quality (results). When the Creative Idea Suggestion System was inaugurated in 1951, the number of suggestions was a mere 789. To increase the number of suggestions, it was necessary to raise the participation of employees in the suggestion system. Accordingly, the Creative Idea committee labored on creative ideas for this problem. As a result of its efforts, the number of suggestions gradually increased, demonstrating that making Creative Idea suggestions has become an established thing for the employees. This period was the growth phase of Toyota's Creative Idea Suggestion System.

One factor responsible for increasing the number of suggestions at Toyota is the element of company culture called "on-site actual checks," described in Chapter One. This means that before judging whether a certain idea will be successful, it is first tried out. To see whether something is suitable for a customer, the first thing is to check out the customer's actual situation. Failures are treated in a positive way, with absolutely no criticism. This principle embodies a tradition extending from the founding of the enterprise, that attaches great importance to the creative spirit.

This principle has been extremely useful in increasing the number of suggestions. To increase quantity, quality must not be ignored. If there is no improvement in the substance of the suggestions and the screening committee decides not to adopt them, those who submitted the suggestions will be discouraged. The next time, the people who wrote the rejected suggestions will lack self-confidence, doubting that their suggestions have a chance, and they will not get involved in suggestion activities.

At Toyota, before the screening committee judges whether the content of a suggestion offers an improvement, the person with the suggestion tries it out on-site. Consequently, by the time the suggestion goes through the screening committee, the substance of it has already been tested, and if it is clear that the suggestion does not offer any improvement, its presentation to the screening committee is discontinued. The content is then reexamined, and supervisors and workers together take up the challenge again. This is an important factor in raising the participation consciousness of the employees toward suggestion activities and in increasing the number of suggestions. Moreover, studying the content of a suggestion also brings about an improvement in quality.

The GI Club

Also in 1974, the Toyota GI (Good Idea) Club was born (treated in detail in Chapter 3). It began as a social club started by 13 people who had received the annual gold prize for excellent suggestions. It was a voluntary group (called an informal group at Toyota) that received no subsidy from the company.

The GI Club began as a group of friends, but through training sessions, lecture meetings, and other activities, it subsequently became a place for self-study for the purpose of making higher quality suggestions in the suggestion activities at the workplace. Currently there are approximately 1000 members. As a voluntary group, its activities take place during off-duty hours, with no remuneration. Continuing these activities would be extremely difficult without the personal commitment of the members.

Managing director Toshimi Onishi, Creative Idea committee vice-chairman, assessed the activities of the GI Club in the following way.

> *It wouldn't be right to say that the GI Club is the Creative Idea Suggestion System, but its members are virtual pros, and are the highest level group in the Creative Idea Suggestion System. The fact is, many of the suggestions by club members at the workplace are excellent, and the GI Club plays an important role in making the Creative Idea Suggestion System so active.*

Currently the GI Club membership is not limited to only gold prize winners ("suggestion pros"), but is organized into three classes including those who seek to become such pros and those with only slight experience with suggestion activities. The club is like a microcosm of Toyota's Creative Idea Suggestion System. The soil that yielded the GI Club existed within the Creative Idea suggestion activities at Toyota. Within that increase in the number of suggestions, there was an increased tendency toward personal commitment among the employees to the suggestion system, a true consciousness of management participation in the process.

The ten years following the birth of the GI Club in 1974 was a period of growth for the Creative Idea Suggestion System, bringing about the improvement in management that was sought when the Creative Idea suggestion activities were introduced.

Moving from an Emphasis on Quantity to an Emphasis on Quality

There is another reason for the development of Toyota's Creative Idea Suggestion System. The analysis by the JHRA also stresses that, "If leadership, staff, or administrators regard suggestions as something extra or as things that some-

Toshimi Onishi,
Vice-chairman
of the Creative Idea
Suggestion Committee

one else should promote, activities will cease." At Toyota, management executives are invariably assigned to the leadership of the Creative Idea committee, which is the highest review committee. Currently, company vice president Tatsuro Toyoda holds the post of chairman of the Creative Idea committee, and managing director Onishi is the committee vice-chairman.

Management, through Onishi, has expressed its position that the Creative Idea Suggestion System is a "pillar of management." The Creative Idea committee secretariat also supports this position. Creative Idea suggestion activities call for a sustained effort, and personnel matters of the secretariat are handled carefully so that few changes are made. As Bando of the Creative Idea secretariat states, "Those in the top echelons of the company are showing pride in the secretariat when they show us that they regard the Creative Idea Suggestion System as a pillar of management."

Creative Idea committee vice-chairman Onishi also explains how top management responds to the suggestion system: "In order for the Creative Idea Suggestion System to take root, it is important that top executives receive suggestions positively. If the top echelons say 'What do we do about this?' to the ideas suggested, then the Creative Idea Suggestion System will not mature."

In 1986, the cumulative total number of suggestions at Toyota passed 15 million, and that number continues to increase.

At Toyota, since the inauguration of the Creative Idea Suggestion System, suggestion activities have been developed principally in the production sector, which is closely linked to cost control. Recently however, many suggestions have come from the administrative section, which has hardly been intimately involved with the suggestion system until now. This is linked to the company-wide effort to increase the quantity of suggestions.

Today, there is a new emphasis on quality, in contrast with suggestion activities that until now have placed great importance on quantity.

The tendency to emphasize quality has already been seen in other companies that have introduced the suggestion system. Although placing importance on quality can improve the economic benefits from suggestions, emphasizing economic results when the suggestion quota cannot be attained can have negative effects, for which managers can be reprimanded. An intensive focus on economic results can destroy morale and wipe out the participative, process-improvement results that have been attained. Furthermore, when there are quotas on the number of suggestions, inevitably only superior suggestions will be submitted, and eventually only "suggestion pros" are involved in suggestion activities.

At Toyota, however, there is sufficient awareness of the problems caused by favoring an emphasis on quality. Accordingly, for new employees with limited experience in suggestion activities, there is a system in which no one asks about quality. For these new employees, an environment is created in which it is easy to participate in suggestion activities. The suggestion activities emphasize improvement in management, which raises an awareness of participation in management, in keeping with the emphasis on quantity.

It was the veteran employees, who have considerable experience with suggestion activities, that thought it would be good for Toyota to turn to an emphasis on quality and quality implementation. As Creative Idea committee vice chairman Onishi states, "I think it is reasonable, after all, for more experienced employees to switch from an emphasis on quantity to one on quality in suggestions. It is necessary to respond to people in a way that corresponds to the development of their ability."

Incidentally, in 1986 when Toyota turned to an emphasis on quality, the number of suggestions per person per year declined slightly. However, Creative Idea committee vice-chairman Onishi is not concerned and believes that this is a temporary phase.

At one time, as previously mentioned, top executives Eiji Toyoda and Shoichi Saito visited the Ford River Rouge plant and studied Ford's suggestion system. In introducing the Creative Idea Suggestion System, which used the Ford system as a model, they sought first to improve the management of the work through the conscious participation of all the employees. Second, they sought to raise economic savings by incorporating improvements in technical and manufacturing areas.

The first step at Toyota was to focus on improving management efficiency through participation and an emphasis on quantity. As a result, the number of suggestions increased by leaps and bounds, and the suggestion system took firm root among the employees. One goal of the Creative Idea

already been achieved, and remains firmly in place. Toyota has now started to pursue the other goal of raising economic efficiency. This accounts for Toyota's turning to an emphasis on quality.

By 1988 the total number of suggestions submitted at Toyota reached 20 million. This was a brilliant achievement for a nearly 40 year-old Creative Idea Suggestion System. On this occasion a commendation program for people who promote excellent suggestions was established by the Creative Idea committee secretariat. This system gives recognition to people whose labors often go unnoticed, although their efforts in the workplace are indispensable for improving the quality of suggestions. By putting them in the limelight Toyota hopes that the quality of suggestions will improve even more.

———

CHAPTER THREE

How the GI Club Supports Suggestion Activities at Toyota

Six Men Who Formed an Elite Creative Idea Group

The Creative Idea Suggestion System involves an annual award system for employees who make outstanding suggestions. Although 40 employees receive a gold prize, 60 a silver prize, and 200 a bronze prize, not even 0.5 percent of all Toyota employees (606,000) actually receive awards. The recipients of these awards succeed in spite of a highly selective system.

There are more than one hundred informal social circles at Toyota. One of these is an elite group called the GI Club, whose membership is limited to a small number of award winners. The club was named for "good idea," a slogan used by the Toyota Creative Idea Suggestion System. Akin to an all-star team in baseball, members cooperate to increase each other's skills and to popularize outstanding suggestions.

Koichi Masuda, managing section chief of the production technology control office, gave the following explanation:

> At Toyota, there are various independent voluntary groups classified according to how their members enter the company. There are social groups for those who enter the company di-

Figure 3-1. Toyota Creative Idea Suggestion System Logo

rectly from high school, and for those who enter after working elsewhere. The company itself has encouraged these activities after learning a lesson from the big strike in 1949. Sometimes board members attend the annual general meeting of these groups as guests. The GI Club is somewhat different from these groups. But the content of its activities is also consistent with company policy, and it is treated by the company in the same way these other groups are treated.

The GI Club, established in 1972, began operating in June 1974. At that time awards in the Toyota Creative Idea Suggestion System were given to a total of 170 persons: 30 gold prize recipients, 40 silver prize recipients and 100 bronze prize recipients. Extra prizes were also awarded: gold and silver recipients got to go on field trips outside the company for three days and two nights, while bronze recipients took one-day trips.

But could the Creative Idea suggestions system grow in a place without the proper soil? In many cases those who made outstanding suggestions were concentrated in one workplace.

Since the field trips then would take key people away from the workplace at the same time, there was a risk of halting the entire assembly line. Extra prize trips were therefore terminated; for 1973, the winners received medals instead.

The last extra prize trips were 1972 visits to the Hiroshima and Yamaguchi factories. Even at that time it was very difficult to win a gold prize. It was not something that was automatic after working for so many hours. Rather, it required wholehearted acceptance of the challenges in one's job everyday, thinking deeply about those challenges, and then writing convincing solutions to problems. Rikio Yamamoto, prize winner in 1972 and first chairman of the GI Club, recalled that he continually submitted more than 50 such suggestions every month.

> *In those days, employees were encouraged to make many suggestions, with the emphasis on quantity rather than quality. I wrote more than 600 suggestions in one year. After finishing work, I would go around the workplace and jot down notes about things I noticed. I wrote down whatever I could right at the workplace. I brought home material about more complicated matters and wrote about them there.*

Since that's what it took to win the prizes, those who went on the prize trips were all high-performance people. That was the first time for some employees to meet each other, although their names had already become well known at other workplaces because of the vigorous role they played in suggestion activities.

In the case of a large-size company like Toyota, even though all the employees belong to the same company, a different factory can seem like a different company. Once a trip was over, fellow employees dispersed and went back to their own workplaces. Barring some extraordinary occurrence, it was unlikely they would meet each other again.

About six months after returning from such a trip, however, Yamamoto was shopping at the Toyota Life Cooperative main store when he met Tsuyoshi Bando once again. Bando (currently a member of the Creative Idea Committee Secretariat) later became the fourth chairman of the GI Club. "That trip was really a lot of fun, wasn't it? Why don't we all get together again sometime?" Yamamoto agreed, and a reunion was planned. It was attended by Yamamoto, Kazuyoshi Kume (second chairman of the GI Club), Seiichi Sakamoto (third chairman), Tsuyoshi Bando, and Masaki Takagi, both of whom at that time were serving as assistant directors of the Creative Idea committee secretariat, and Noboru Ibi. This was the "Group of Six," which was the predecessor of the GI Club.

The GI Club's Mutual Enlightenment Through Suggestion Activities

Bando can still remember the details of his conversation with Yamamoto in the Life Cooperative store. Yamamoto joked that Bando was the founder, so Bando nominated Yamamoto as the first chairman. Once every two months they used to visit each other's homes, and the friendship groups evolved in this manner as they shared homemade meals together, purchased with group "dues" of ¥1000 ($7.50) per person. Yamamoto reminisces:

> *I was fascinated by the deep level of communication that resulted from a chance encounter between two people. There were some times when we stayed up late drinking together for three nights in a row. At first, our conversations focused on our hobbies, but each of the six people was a kind of "king of the mountain." We were all strong individualists, so when there was an argument, you wondered whether the group was on the verge of self-destructing.*

As meetings went on, the members began to think, "It's a shame that after going to all the trouble to have these meetings, only six people can attend them. If the company offered to pay for our trips, we could earn cash awards for creative ideas and then plan the trips ourselves." The call for participation by other gold prize winners began around the time when the groups finished a round of visits to the six members' homes. Thirteen gold medalists responded to the invitation. When they all met in June 1974 at the Suigen clubroom in the Welfare Facilities Building near the company headquarters factory, the Toyota GI Club was born.

One of the Group of Six, Kazuyoshi Kume, began by saying: "An association whose purpose is only for its members to drink together is pointless. I think we should give talks about improvement examples." These words foreshadowed the direction of the GI Club as it aimed at mutual enlightenment through suggestion activities.

The GI Club is defined in club rules as "an independent association of persons who study creative ideas," with its main office under the auspices of the Creative Idea committee secretariat. Being a Toyota Motor Company employee is a primary qualification for joining the club. Originally, only gold prize recipients could join, but in 1977, this was broadened to include bronze prize recipients. Sadanori Oyama, the 1989 GI Club auditor, remarks: "Since the president's award goes only to gold prize recipients, and those who receive silver prizes or less only get certificates of merit, the gold prize is a formidable attainment in suggestion activities."

The scope of in-house improvements was broadened during 1976. When it became desirable to increase the number of those who make excellent suggestions, chapters of the GI Club were started in areas such as machining, press working, assembly, and so on, at each workplace. Currently, 20 subcommittees have been established, and 360 employees belong to chapters at company headquarters. Anyone with an interest in suggestion activities can participate in chapters, even employees who are not prize winners. The number of company employees participating in subcommittees is close to 1000.

The current chairman, Kiyokazu Kodama, smiled broadly as he said: "Chapters also function independently now. If anything, they have grown to a point where they are at least as active as the main GI Club at company headquarters." Expenses for activities are covered by dues income of ¥20 million ($150,000). The chapters receive no financial support at all from the company and fund their own year-end parties.

The following are chapter rules:

1. The purpose of these chapters is to contribute to the expansion of the company through suggestion activities, while at the same time fostering friendship among chapter members and self-enlightenment through Creative Idea suggestion activities.
2. The following measures are to be implemented to achieve the goals of these chapters:
   a. Establishing study groups to popularize and apply outstanding suggestion examples.
   b. Establishing lecture classes to increase suggestion activities.
   c. Establishing training groups and seminars to promote exchanges among chapter members.
   d. Doing whatever else is necessary to achieve the goals of the chapter.

One of the most important GI Club activities is establishing study groups, in which chapter members give an average of four talks a month about outstanding suggestions. This stimulates debate among all participating members, and suggestions are further refined: "It would have been better if you did this that way," or "If you do that this way, we could have saved ¥4000 instead of ¥3000."

After improvement examples have been implemented at a workplace and then improved by debate, the participants bring them back to their own workplaces for further on-site development, and participants can then speak about the suggestions with familiarity and considerable authority.

By fiscal 1987, it became clear that when an example from a very different kind of work was used at lecture meetings, it was difficult for workers unfamiliar with the work to understand despite the effort put into presenting it. This was an obstacle to the horizontal flow of know-how between departments in different plants. Things were therefore reorganized in fiscal 1988 and information and examples were shared according to shops or type of work, with people in assembly studying about assembly and those in machining studying about machining.

GI Club Study Group for Publicizing Examples

The GI Club's Many Activities in the Company

Much of the GI Club's influence comes from its efforts to promote suggestion activities. In 1978, when the GI Club had just begun to take root in the company, 28 of the 32 three-consecutive-year prize winners were members of the GI Club. The third year is said to be the hardest for getting this prize. Tsuyoshi Bando explained the reason:

> *If you become a person who makes suggestions excellent enough to receive this prize, you still remain at the workplace doing your usual job. To cultivate leadership talent among your subordinates, you have to handle things in such a way that subordinates are allowed to get the prize instead of you. Even if the material is something that you yourself have researched, there are times when you must let the prize go to subordinates to encourage their development.*

In the words of Ryoji Mori of the GI Club: "The 'environment' plays a major role in the making of good suggestions, even in the case of managers." Mori began by getting a bronze prize in 1984 and then won three gold prizes in 1985, 1986, and 1987. In 1986 he received the three-consecutive-year prize. Mori recalled some of his strong impressions:

> *When I was working in my former position, I knew about the existence of the Creative Idea Suggestion System, but there were few people around me who had a good understanding of it. The common wisdom at that workplace was that it was okay to be only superficially involved in the suggestion system. However, the component section was established three years ago, and when I was assigned to it, my boss was a man who had a good understanding of the Creative Idea Suggestion System. That boss used to stress the fact that quality and price objectives could never be*

achieved unless improvements were made. At that time I thought I had run into a really amazing man.

Kiyokazu Kodama, the current chairman of the GI Club, also had similar experiences in regard to managers. As he put it:

> At a time when I didn't know what to write on suggestion forms, or how I should write it, my foreman chided me that I wasn't trying hard enough to write suggestions. Anyway, I began writing them. That was how my suggestion writing career began. My foreman always praised the good points of my suggestions, but never pointed out the bad ones.
>
> It wasn't until later that I noticed that my foreman had not tried to point out my bad points. Anyway, I think it was around that time that I first received a bronze prize. At that time, my family must have wondered, "What is Kiyokazu so intent on writing every Sunday?" As things turned out, my supervisors praised me and kept asking me to win a prize "one more year," so I kept it up for three years!"

Mori's boss and Kodama's boss were also members of the GI Club. It is easy to imagine that the GI Club is a place for fostering leadership qualities. It should also be noted that GI Club activities, sponsored by each chapter, function as classes for teaching new company recruits how to write suggestion forms. Even for the same suggestion, there are differences in evaluations for "before improvement," "after improvement," and "benefits" since a third person reads them and makes notations using Japanese characters.

"How can you write the most convincingly on a single sheet of paper?" Lectures are given to answer that question, based on the experience and performance of those who have made outstanding suggestions. The purpose of the writing methods classes is to have the company's new recruits master the art of writing properly, and there are absolutely no prerequisites for participating.

Participants in the writing methods classes use a handwritten text, the *Creative Idea Guide*, subtitled, "Aiming to Build a Workplace That Makes Your Life and Your Work Worthwhile!" Among the topics covered are: the proper attitude when making suggestions, what to aim at in matters of quality, safety costs, and labor-hours, methods of calculating improvement benefits, and specific methods of filling in suggestion forms. While comparing examples of past suggestions with these, lecture classes make progress by teaching participants to stop making excuses such as, "If you write that, people will laugh at you," "It's technically unfeasible," "It costs too much," or "That's outdated."

The following are some other GI Club activities.

- Holding field trips to other factories and exchanging meetings.
- Holding study group meetings and lecture classes.
- Holding discussions after field trips.
- Participating in external organizations to present the results of projects.

To date there have been exchange meetings with the Creative Idea circles of other companies and participation in horizontal Creative Idea groups for presenting talks on research papers at each company. There have also been activities such as field trips at the chapter level to Cheju Island (a resort in Korea).

At other companies, writing method classrooms or horizontal development toward other workplaces through groups for giving talks about examples almost always are the work of Creative Idea secretariats (improvement secretariats). That the GI Club, which grew out of a single autonomous activities circle, pooled its own members' money and seriously accepted the challenges involved should give some idea of Toyota's

Current Situation	Improvement Idea	Benefits
Level 1 I perform the _____ installation operation according to the following steps: 1 _____ , 2 _____ , 3 _____ . _____ has occurred.	I changed the _____ installation operation as follows: 1 _____ , 2 _____ , 3 _____ .	1. The occurrence of _____ was eliminated. 2. _____ has improved.
Level 2 I perform the _____ installation operation according to the following steps: 1 _____ , 2 _____ , 3 _____ . _____ has occurred. The _____ defect occurs _____ times each day, and _____ has happened so many times.	I changed the _____ installation operation as follows: 1 _____ , 2 _____ , 3 _____ . Before Improvement: 1 ____ 2 ____ 3 ____ After Improvement: 1 ____ 2 ____ 3 ____ "before" sketch "after" sketch	1. The occurrence of _____ became _____ . 2. The _____ improved to _____ extent. 3. The _____ also improved.
Level 3 I install _____ in the installation process for _____ , but there are the following problems: 1. A defect in _____ occurred _____ . 2. The _____ is bad; _____ and _____ occurred. 3. The _____ is also bad; _____ occurred.	By doing _____ and _____ to _____ , the problems were solved. Before Improvement: 1 ____ 2 ____ 3 ____ After Improvement: 1 ____ 2 ____ 3 ____ "before" sketch "after" sketch	1. _____ defects were reduced by _____ . 2. The _____ improved; _____ per _____ reduction 3. By improving _____ , _____ became possible and _____ became possible. 4. The _____ operation was stabilized. Even _____ can use this method.

Note: By making it possible to use any of the above three formats, technical skills are improved.

Figure 3-2. Filling Out GI Club Creative Idea Suggestion Forms

1. Reducing work overlapping labor-hours

Cost reduction = A × B × C × D × E

A = overlap frequency
B = time required for one time
C = day/night
D = number of days operated in one month
E = labor cost per hour

2. Efficiency of reducing labor-hours for machinery maintenance

Cost reduction = A × B × C

Efficiency is improved by entering various factors into the calculation, such as overtime resulting from breakdowns that cause work slowdowns

Cost reduction = A × B × C × D

A = down time due to accidents, etc.
B = maintenance personnel
C = labor costs per hour
D = overtime due to operation slowdown

3. Efficiency of reducing cutter costs

Cost reduction = A × B

A = cutter unit price
B = number of monthly damage reduction cases

4. Efficiency of prolonging cutter life span

Amount per unit (E) = (A ÷ B) − (A ÷ C)
Cost reduction = E × D

A = cutter unit price
B = number of processes
C = number of process changeovers
D = number of units per month

5. Efficiency of improving assembly operations (reducing the number of steps walked by changing locations of parts areas)

Number of seconds reduced per unit = A × B
Monthly labor-hour reduction (yen) = D × E ÷ 3600 × C

A = number of steps
B = calculation on basis of one step per second
C = number of units produced per month
D = labor costs per hour
E = number of seconds reduced per unit

Figure 3-3. Calculating the Benefits of Creative Idea Suggestions

enterprising climate and the latent energy within its Creative Idea Suggestion System.

Personal Experiences of GI Club Members

So far, we have simply described the GI Club's contributions to the company through its activities and its fostering of leadership. But for specific suggestion activities of the GI Club, things can be explained more effectively through the personal experiences of club members. Here is what three of them had to say.

My Enthusiasm for the GI Club
by Takao Umezu,
Kamigo factory, second machining division
(sixth chairman of the GI Club)

"Just a minute, Mr. Umezu. Do you have any free time later on today? If you don't mind, I'd like to see you about something."

This is what my foreman said to me one day as I was getting ready to go home. This man had never spoken to me outside of a work situation.

I wondered if he was going to take me out to eat, and deep in my heart I really hoped he would. So I answered with an enthusiastic yes. But I was completely disappointed. The place we arrived at was not a restaurant or a yakitori shop. It was a place I had never heard of, a hall with a sign that read "Second Toyota GI Club Example Exchange Meeting." I was disappointed, but since I had agreed to go, I could hardly turn back now, so I reluctantly went in and took a seat.

I was amazed when I happened to look toward the front of the hall where the presenters were seated. One of the people seated there was someone who had been a year behind me during my high school days. We had belonged to the same club during our school days and he had been friendly to me. And now here he was, about to give a talk to members of the Toyota GI Club who had come together here from all the Toyota factories. As I began to think about this situation, I supposed that what had happened so far had been arranged by my foreman, and before I knew it, my feelings of disappointment vanished.

Finally, it was my friend's turn to speak. At that point, my heart began to beat faster, just as though I were the one giving the talk. When he began to speak, I was surprised again. The content of his improvement suggestion was impressive, and the charts he used were works of art, something that I could never have made myself. His delivery was consistently good.

I hadn't realized he was so talented. After hearing his talk, I was struck by a sense of my own worthlessness and I lost any sense of being superior to him because I was a year ahead of him in school. I felt that it would be great to be able to implement the kind of change he had talked about. So far, I had had it too easy.

I could not bring myself to talk with him that day, so I finally left, trying to get away before he noticed me. From that time on, I made a firm decision that I would also participate in Creative Idea suggestion activities. I had been very much stimulated by that meeting for publicizing ideas, and I was somewhat humiliated that my younger friend was so far ahead of me in suggestion activities. From then on, I used to walk around my workplace, searching intently for anything that might provide material for a Creative Idea suggestion.

But the harder you think about this, the more you fail to come up with improvement ideas, and not even a single idea occurs to you. It was on such a day that my foreman summoned me once again and gave me the following advice:

> *In the beginning it's pointless to set your sights on some grand scheme. You'll find plenty of material for creative ideas*

in the "4S:" arranging things properly, keeping them in order, neatness, and cleanliness. The first thing to do is to apply 4S to the area right around you. You can find lots of material for creative ideas right there. Things you dislike, things that are dangerous or hard to do – anything is okay. A creative idea means changing a troublesome situation into a trouble-free situation. Anyone at all who keeps on making small improvements is capable of making big improvements.

But even though I understood the idea behind what he was saying, I just couldn't find anything to be improved. My foreman came over to me again while I was working, perhaps because he couldn't stand to see me in such a hurry all the time, and suddenly scolded me in a loud voice: "Hey, is that work hard to do?" To tell the truth, it really was. But I had simply gotten used to the fact that it was hard to do. Did that loud voice suggest material for making a suggestion? On the following day, I suggested to my foreman that if a certain kind of tool were used, the work would become easier to do, and he made arrangements for it right away. The result was that the work became much easier to do, and there were no more situations in which we were pressed for time.

However, I could relax only for a short time. The next thing my foreman said to me was, "By the way, have you filled out the suggestion form? No matter how hard you try to make an improvement, there just won't be any unless you fill out the suggestion form." It was only a matter of a single page, but I did not know how to fill it out, so I spent all night working on it. Although I felt apprehensive about it, I submitted it to my foreman the next morning. But he said, "Oh, this is good. You've really done a good job writing this up." Because of his words, I was no longer apprehensive. From then on, I had a lot of confidence in myself. The first cash award I received was only ¥500 (less than $5), but it made me extremely happy.

A few days later, as I was continuing to make several improvements, I ran into a problem that my idea alone could not solve, so I consulted with my foreman. He gave me some advice about it, saying "Umezu, this problem has deep roots, but it looks as though it is worth tackling. If it can be solved, it would result in making a great improvement."

After implementing the improvement and verifying the results, I quickly filled out the suggestion form. But my foreman's reaction was unfavorable. He rejected it, saying:

> You can't let yourself relax when writing up this kind of good suggestion. Unless the quality of the form corresponds to the suggestion content, people on the screening committee will not understand it well and you will not be able to get the kind of evaluation you want. But if you write it up well, you'll win ¥3000 ($23). What about the current situation? What was causing the trouble? What methods should be used to solve the problem points? How much will this cost? What about benefits? Can you show how much money will be saved? And there should probably be other areas that become more efficient as a result. Those are the things you have to write down.

I never felt time pass as slowly as it seemed to between the time I handed in my suggestion form and the time I received my cash award. The prize money I received two months later was ¥4000, ¥1000 more than I had expected.

This experience provided me with the opportunity to realize the importance of properly filling out suggestion forms and to grasp the meaning of improvement objectives. I came to realize the value of creative ideas when I was submitting more than 200 suggestions per year.

It had become one of my daily routines, on getting home from work, to take out the notes I had jotted down while working and place a suggestion form in front of me. When I made excuses for my laziness, such as "I'm tired today, so I think I'll do it tomorrow," my wife would say, "Have you already finished this month's quota?"

I received the bronze prize I had wanted so badly three years after being humiliated by my friend's presentation. When someone at the workplace makes an excellent suggestion, colleagues who also work in the same area are fired up with the desire not to lag behind. This is rivalry in the good sense of the word, transforming the workplace into a more active place. When I received the three consecutive year prize, my wife, who was also working for Toyota at the time, was overjoyed.

I joined the GI Club the same year that I won the bronze prize. At first I remained just a young man who was in over his head, even though the name of each member was recognized at every factory as the name of a talented person. I never felt comfortable and confident, but as time went on, I was guided by more experienced members and given more and more significant roles to play (I served as chairman in 1985). I tried as hard as I could not to let them down. Consequently, I was promoted to group leader, the highest position attained by anyone among those who entered the company the same time I did.

Late at night, while drinking tea that my wife had poured for me, I had a suggestion form in front of me. Maybe it was a scene like this that my child tried to describe in a primary school composition, "My Wonderful Papa." As you might expect, I was deeply moved when I saw this composition. I remember being taught by a little child when I read the words, "It is important for leaders to take the initiative."

My Feelings about Improvement
by Akihiko Hasegawa,
general assembly division, company headquarters factory
(a vice-chairman of the GI Club in 1989)

"You are qualified for machine design" – that's what I, who had been assigned to maintenance, hoped to hear when I joined the company. At the actual workplace, however, the only work I did was that of a metal worker, making things such as hoisting accessories, applying paint every day to boxes and shelves I had welded together.

Furthermore, because of a shortage of workers caused by constantly increasing line production, for about half a week the maintenance workers had to help out on the line. We would rush over to help in one area on Monday and then in another on Tuesday. When I had finished doing a job, someone would call out to me, "Hey, wait! You're from maintenance, aren't you? Please fix this." Since I did not yet have much maintenance knowledge or technical skill, the only thing I could do was hurry back to where I usually worked and get help from more experienced colleagues. Those were days when it really dawned on me how little skill I had.

It shouldn't have turned out this way. I watched new recruits and colleagues in my area leaving the company one after another, maybe because they shared my sentiments. So I had a heart-to-heart talk with my foreman. As he put it: "You still had it easier than I did. In my day, we had to help out here and there for a certain number of hours. But when I think about it now, I realize that the experience I gained on the line at that time helped me a lot with my current job."

One day this same foreman called out to me: "The line is having a hard time handling crossties stained with oil. How about your trying to improve the situation? Anyway, take a look at it." And that was all he said. The crossties on the line are wooden blocks used for mounting frames on the conveyor.

The person in charge at the beginning of the line mounts one block at a time on the conveyor. At the end of the line, another person keeps taking the blocks off, one at a time. I have also had experience helping them out there, and it really is a very troublesome operation, getting your hands very dirty from the oil. I thought maybe we could find a way to use machines for this operation, and I got advice from my colleagues. Somehow we managed to work things out. After coaching from my foreman, I submitted my first suggestion.

One morning, two months later, I heard my foreman shouting "Hey, Hasegawa!" My first reaction was to suspect that he was going to send me somewhere to help out again. But, something seemed different this time. I was surprised when he told me, "You've done a good job. That was really an outstanding suggestion."

I used the award money to buy sweet cakes. And I'll never forget how they tasted as I shared them with all my colleagues.

From that time on, whenever I was sent somewhere to help out, it was just the way my foreman said it would be. I came to think of such an experience as a "training ground" and became much more eager to acquire qualifications needed for my job. So far, I have managed to acquire on my own 15 different kinds of qualifications and certificates, some of them in-house and some of them outside the company. "There is a yearly prize system for creative ideas and 300 employees throughout the company can receive prizes," said my foreman. "You're talented enough, why don't you try competing for one of these prizes?" My performance got better as time went by and the number of my suggestions steadily increased.

One day my foreman gave me the following advice: "Why don't you keep an improvement diary and make suggestions in a more organized way?" I decided to walk around the line area at least twice a day, look for material, think of improvements, and continue to submit suggestions. But my foreman's guidelines for filling out suggestion forms gradually became stricter and stricter. While working on a suggestion, there were many times I thought there was no point in going on. At those times he kept on telling me how important it was to make on-site investigations and gather lots of new information from the assembly line. And he drove home to me the importance of getting advice from supervisors and more experienced colleagues, while considering matters of cost, quality, and safety from many different perspectives.

I finally received a gold prize in 1981, and I received a three consecutive year prize. My prize-winning triggered a situation that stimulated my colleagues and subordinates so that we were winning prizes regularly every year; this resulted in our workplace winning an award in 1984 for being an outstanding workplace.

I joined the GI Club as soon as I received my first prize. In 1985 I started a subcommittee at my own workplace. In 1987 and 1988 I was on the company headquarters executive committee, and in 1986 I was promoted to group leader.

When there is some request from the line at the workplace, I call my subordinates more and more frequently, telling them, "Hey, everyone assemble over here, we're going to the workplace. I don't have any good ideas, but I want all of you to tell me about yours." I was making steady progress, step by step, as a small group activities leader.

Later on, however, everything was not such smooth sailing. There are all kinds of people at a workplace and it is not so easy to build good human relations among them. "Don't put on airs, saying this or that, just because you're a group leader." This is what two senior workers said who had come over from the assembly line to the maintenance area. I was stunned by this and I can remember inadvertently bowing my head as they spoke these words while glaring at me. I was completely at a loss as to how to handle this situation. The attitudes of these older workers regarding my leadership deficiencies also had an effect on our suggestion activities as workplace morale kept getting lower.

Looking for some way of making our workplace more active again, I tried hard to cultivate friendship among fellow workers, arranging things such as two-day fishing trips with an overnight stay. And then something happened that provided an opportunity to change the situation decisively for the better. A conference was held in which someone suggested, "When six nuts are required for a job, it is inefficient to count them one by one. Doesn't someone have a good idea which would allow six nuts at a time to be provided?" At the end of a period of trial and error, construction of a machine in which the principle of a pachinko ball changer was applied had been 80 percent completed. But the electrical circuit wiring was a problem. To my surprise, however, those two older workers who had scolded me had worked together with their subordinates and made countless tests for this difficult operation. When they brought the completed machine a week later, saying "Group leader, we did it!," I was deeply moved. And later on, workplace creative ideas gradually increased over previous levels because of the accomplishments of many workers, including those two older workers, who devised a hoist hook rotary return that would not require any additional cost. Suggestion activities had become a lubricant for human relations.

Creative Ideas and Making the Workplace More Active
by Hideaki Murase, general assembly division,
Tsutsumi factory

I was repeatedly absent from work on short notice. I had no enthusiasm for my work at all, and I did only the minimum requirements of my job. A few years after joining the company, I thought that such things as improvements were things to be done by others. Since I had no spirit of cooperation, I was moved around to different factories and workplaces, and of course I had no record of making suggestions at all. The turning point for me came five years after joining the company at a time when I was assigned to the assembly line. What on earth were those guys writing down so intently? While I thought about how I should react to what they were doing, all the workers on the assembly line were filled with enthusiasm. They saved up their Creative Idea prize money and actively supported social functions and parties to encourage communication among workers. The group leader called out to me, "Hey, Murase, next week is the deadline for creative ideas. Give us your suggestion this month!" When I responded, "I want to submit a suggestion, but I don't have a form, so I can't," I was rebelling childishly. I had received only the forms for the results of the previous month, so I used this as an excuse.

The group leader then said, "Oh, is that so? Well then, let me give you some forms." His rejoinder was only natural. He handed over 30 forms to me, a person who had no record at all of making suggestions. Deep in my heart, I knew he was calling my bluff, but the damage had already been done. After I got back home, I racked my brains with the suggestion form in front of me, but I just didn't get any ideas at all. At that time, one sheet of paper fell out from between the suggestion forms. Several improvement examples were printed together on that sheet, such as improvement objectives and methods, methods of filling out forms, calculating efficiency, and so on. "Ah, my group leader." Not only had he given me suggestion materials, but he was also watching over me without being pretentious about it. I felt like bowing to him out of respect.

On the next day, after the lights had been turned off and everyone had gone home, I walked around the dark workplace with a flashlight in one hand and a memo pad in the other. I spent the whole night filling out the suggestion form. This was the first step turning point that changed my life in the company.

Actually, I didn't know much about improvements at all and I had knowledge about only one process operation. The best I could do was to submit five suggestions a month. I knew my group leader was concerned about this, but ideas were just not coming to me.

I therefore established a schedule for thinking about "opposite" ways to do things an hour before starting work, and I always worked at my desk after getting back home. I had accepted the challenge of writing up one suggestion per day.

A short time after that, I responded to a special call for suggestions in our section and finally won an individual's prize, my first since joining the company. At that time, straight line production was necessary at the production site because of the oil crisis. A pall of stagnation hung heavily in the company atmosphere at the height of the period when everyone knew the pain of being without work. After that, I set higher goals for myself and even won a gold prize. Even now, I can never forget how deeply moved I was at the award ceremony. My father was even happier than I was. He said to me, "Hideaki, I've worked at Toyota for 40 years, but I've never won a president's prize or anything like that. You have done it instead of me, and you've given me something very precious." I have never felt such a sense of satisfaction as I did on seeing my aging father's tears of joy.

When I received the gold prize, I joined the GI Club. Of course I was challenged by outstanding colleagues and my competitive spirit was aroused. I was also greatly surprised by the fact that younger colleagues were being trained at the workplaces of club members. Stimulated by such colleagues, I threw myself into things wholeheartedly, hoping that my contributions would be recognized by everyone else and that I would become the best suggestion maker at Toyota. Whenever I noticed a problem, I immediately jotted it down in my notebook. Using my spare time carefully, I would then try out some solution. And there were many times when I talked things over with my colleagues in the GI Club.

My wife served me coffee even very late at night. And when my children, who had less time with me because of my night work, saw my certificates and medals, one of them said: "Daddy's awards look really impressive, don't they? When I grow up, I'm going to get a prize too." And then they imitated me filling out suggestion forms. I enjoyed the warm support of my whole family. I was awarded the company prize for five consecutive years beginning in 1979.

My self-confidence increased a lot as a result of receiving the three consecutive year prize during a period of suggestion activities that we had been trying hard to improve each year. That was around the time we managed to get over the oil crisis and restore double-line production. I then had to leave the group leader who had introduced me to the joy of suggestion activities, as well as the colleagues whose trials I had shared, for I had been appointed the leader of a new workplace, responsible for workplace management.

But it was not easy to begin working as a group leader. I was not a very effective leader, and I lacked a feeling of solidarity with people at the workplace.

So instead of improved performance, the results were just the opposite. Whatever countermeasures I proposed were hard to get accepted. Since I had wanted very much to become a group leader, the only thing I really got excited about was improving our performance. I realized that I had ignored work processes and I reflected on my behavior so far. I then tried to stimulate the workplace through small group activities such as Creative Idea suggestion activities.

I went around explaining how wonderful the Creative Idea Suggestion System was, while guiding workers in how to dig up material and showing them what to look for. I also explained to them on-site actual processes, telling them, "If you come up with a creative idea, your own work gets easier to do, you receive a higher evaluation, and you can receive a cash award. It's a golden opportunity to make an appeal to many other workers." There was some opposition among the younger workers, some of them saying "I disagree with you," and there were some who submitted only major suggestions whose efficiency was difficult to estimate. But I gradually overcame the difficulties, explaining individually to each person how efficient it was to contribute a constant stream of small suggestions.

I do not use the suggestion forms that are submitted exclusively for creative ideas. For example, when we discover people who draw pictures well, we provide lettering training and a place for their activities. We make good use of their individuality by giving them vigorous bottom-up training. I personally study each suggestion form and the forms help me guide my subordinates.

Is this approach effective? Two of my subordinates were trained as group leaders, and before long I was promoted to foreman. Shortly after that, the Japanese economy was struggling under the burden of a rapidly appreciating yen. And in the case of Creative Idea activities, many were calling for a change from quantity to quality. But somehow this challenge was also met successfully, by strengthening ties of solidarity with other workplaces and by responding with improvements that were immediately effective.

I have already mentioned how my group leader gave me 30 suggestion forms at a time when I was frequently absent from work on short notice, and indifferent toward my job. And I also described how, since that time, I have been very enthusiastic about creative ideas while improving myself. In the future, I hope to assiduously maintain the foundation of the gift given to me by my supervisors, Creative Idea suggestion activities. And I hope to improve the creative ideas of the workplace by making the environment there more stimulating.

Why Make Suggestions?

There are various reasons for joining the GI Club, depending on who you ask. But one of the most common motivations seems to be an invitation from one's superiors after winning an award. Masami Watanabe, the seventh chairman of the GI Club, joined the club in 1977. The main reason was that he had been invited to do so by a manager he had met while on a prize trip after winning a bronze prize in 1972. Thinking back about those days, Watanabe said:

> I had heard stories about a club whose members were all extraordinary people. On joining this club, I was completely won over. After entering the club, I had less time to devote to private matters, but the experience of being challenged by talented people was definitely a plus when I had to give guidance to workers. The fact of the matter is that before I was appointed chairman, I had gone through the ranks with accounting and vice-chairman positions. These positions were obscure, but valuable as a means of activating the workplace.

The truth is, however, that Watanabe was also one of those employees who had absolutely no interest in creative ideas when he joined the company. As Watanabe put it:

> I have been working at Toyota for 20 years, but I never even looked at a suggestion form during my first five years. To make up for that time, I submitted an average of about 10

suggestions per month, but so far I have submitted a total of 2400 suggestions. I suppose one of the reasons was a feeling of satisfaction that a suggestion of mine was being used at the workplace. And it also really made me happy when company brass came to see the result and asked, "Who's responsible for this improvement?" It felt good when the answer was, "Watanabe is."

The following are some of the impressions of Sadonori Oyama (GI Club auditor in 1989) when he joined the club:

Although there were no rules for attending meetings, I saw people frequently going to meetings, coming from distant workplaces as soon as work was over. I thought to myself that they must certainly be learning something worthwhile at the meetings. However, it was not what I had imagined. Studying and making progress were matters of personal initiative, and it was impossible to go on without constantly developing an awareness of new problems. You cannot belong to this club unless you have solid convictions of your own.

There is something ironic about a man like Oyama writing in the club bulletin, "Those who have high expectations of getting something by entering this club should withdraw from it immediately."

Each member of the GI Club is a creative idea "professional," but at first, everyone goes through a beginner's stage. Before they become real pros, they do a lot of thinking about suggestion activities and that motivates them to join. From an outside perspective, it might look like stubbornness and tenacity, simply the desire to gain prize money. But Tsuyoshi Bando strongly disagrees that money is a key motivation:

Although cash awards are indeed made, everybody knows the amount of money involved, and it is just not something that anyone would continue doing for the money. It is rather a matter of wanting to improve oneself. The fundamental reasons why people persevere in suggestion activities are to improve themselves, to become group leaders quickly, and to get earlier assignments to foremen positions. While thinking about what they can do to get faster promotions, they develop an awareness of problems related to their jobs and make suggestions, eventually earning incremental ¥100 raises and promotions. Advancement and these raises give people an indescribable sense of satisfaction and abundance.

In my case, I joined the company after leaving another company. As I found myself working with colleagues younger than myself, I wanted to become a supervisor quickly. I wanted to catch up with others fast. And it was not just a matter of taking no days off, showing up for work, and working as hard as I could. Somehow I wanted to show that I was more skilled than others. And that's why I continued to throw myself wholeheartedly into suggestion activities.

Using Talent That Cannot Be Used on the Job

The first chairman of the GI Club, Rikio Yamamoto, also joined Toyota after leaving another company. He expressed similar sentiments:

It was the year when a typhoon struck Ise harbor. I can still remember my thoughts when I was asked at an interview, "You have no objections to being a temporary employee indefinitely?" and responding, "No problem, that's fine with me." I joined the company and was assigned to an assembly line at a time when suggestion activities were conducted hurriedly by group leaders and foremen. Somehow I wanted people to recognize the fact that Rikio Yamamoto was now on the assembly line, so I forced myself to write suggestions. That was also a time when I would lash out at the secretariat when my suggestions were rejected, demanding to know why they were rejected in spite of all the research I did on problem points and in spite of the improvements made. I would ask them to come to the workplace; I didn't want them evaluating my suggestions while sitting at their desks.

Although he had a bit of a chip on his shoulder, Yamamoto won a gold prize in 1972. In 1975, he received the Prefectural Science and Technology Prize. In 1981 he was given the Distinguished Employee award on the occasion of the Creative Idea Suggestion System's thirtieth anniversary.

The Prefectural Science and Technology Prize is for suggestions whose cash awards amount to ¥20,000 ($150) or more. The company makes a petition through the prefectural office to the science and technology office, where an evaluation is made. It is therefore a prize that confers honor on the outstanding person who receives it. In 1988 there were 800 people who received this award throughout Japan. Seventeen of those people were Toyota employees.

There was still another incident involving Yamamoto. There are currently 40 gold prize winners, but there were 30 until the Creative Idea Suggestion System was revised in 1976. The person who was responsible for increasing the number by ten was Yamamoto. It happened after the factory director came to ask Yamamoto why there were so many gold prize winners in his section.

When I was foreman, 27 of the 30 people who won gold prizes were from my section. At that time, I was summoned by the factory director; he was all upset. He said, "I'm not criticizing you, but it makes problems when a single section monopolizes the winning of prizes." I was at a loss about what to do when he said this to me. To keep an overall balance, there wasn't anything else I could do other than increase the number of possible prize recipients.

When it's a matter of reforming the system, you have to go beyond the level of section and division managers and get involved with the company directors. Consequently, there was some debate about reforming a system that had been put together by the high-ranking members of the Creative Idea committee. On the other hand, in those days I was happy about the achievements of my section and I remember thinking that we had done something of great significance.

At that time, computers and robots were not very advanced. Yamamoto continued to explain his "secret":

One day, as we were making some rather crude improvements on the assembly line, such as changing driving positions from right to left for the United States market, Taiichi Ohno, called the father of the Toyota production system, came over and spoke to us. He told us, "Making improvements in the maintenance and machine divisions results in major efficiency. But since the assembly line is a place where small parts are handled, there may not be so much material for improvement. However, you've done a good job by making real improvements on the assembly line." Morale at our workplace soared after hearing those words, and workers kept finding more and more material for improvement.

What clearly emerges from these statements is that the Creative Idea Suggestion System requires individual efforts. It is like a special tool whose value needs to be recognized by those who encounter it.

At workplaces where there are many typical standard line operations, decisions about work are always made on a large scale. Suggestions dealing with a situation like this can thus have a large effect, depending on the ideas and observation powers of those who make them. That is precisely why when a person's own strengths are inadequate for doing the job assigned, suggestions will help the person to do more than an adequate job and will also result in a higher evaluation.

Yamamoto, who had been promoted from a temporary worker to factory director, and who was called by his colleagues a man of exceptional ability and luck, had this to say: "That the suggestion system affects how workers are evaluated causes some problems, but it is a fact that reference is made to these evaluations. When the whistle blows, most employees wash their hands and promptly return home. When I notice one person at his desk during that time filling out the suggestion form before him, I am deeply impressed." The system's emphasis on stresses a person's individuality and provides opportunities for promotion is accurately described in the notes and memoranda of GI Club members.

The GI Club Goes Overseas

As soon as any of Toyota's more than 30 overseas production factories was completed, expert workplace managers from Japan were sent there. They then proceeded to make improvements and adjustments in the equipment and production system. These overseas assignments were divided into two types: long-term "residence" and short-term "support." Looking after the entire production system of a factory was an assignment involving "residence." In addition, to raise the level of skills for each section, it is necessary to make various detailed improvements for each position. When such improvements are required, "support" people are sent from factories in Japan to implement them.

One of Toyota's branches in Indonesia was a company called PH Toyota-Mobilindo, where 860 employees produced things such as truck beds and deck frames for commercial vehicles. They supplied these to another company in Indonesia,

PT Astra (in January 1989, the two companies merged, with Astra Co. as the successor company). Masami Watanabe was in residence at Mobilindo from 1982 for 27 months as the person in charge of press and maintenance improvements. Watanabe's mission there was to provide overall guidance for suggestion activities and QC circle activities. He trained workers until he was able to solve a problem situation in which suggestions were being made at the rate of five per person per year and all QC circles had two topics per year.

Watanabe spoke as though it was only natural to do work that was outside the scope of one's regular job:

> *I thought long and hard about what kind of extra work I might be able to do outside of my regular job. It would be a shame if people referred to me as that guy who didn't do anything at all except his regular job, wouldn't it? When I happened to think about it, the fact remained that I was a member of the GI Club, a person confident of success in matters involving knowledge of creative ideas. And about six months after I took up my new assignment, I moved into the implementation stage.*

Before Watanabe began his new assignment, there had been several thousand suggestions made at Mobilindo. But the system itself was not clearly defined, and it seems that even workers at the workplace did not understand what a "problem" was. At any rate, they were not collecting any data at all right at the workplace. Consequently, they had no grasp at all of how many defective goods were being turned out each day nor of how many good products were being made. A system was therefore installed in which data were collected once a day so that everyone understood at a glance what the defective rate was. A method of management was introduced that encouraged competition among sections.

At the same time, creative idea training was started and excellent suggestions began to be submitted. When a suggestion is praised by one's supervisors, a person is encouraged and thinks, "Okay then, I'll submit another one." Watanabe introduced people who had submitted outstanding suggestions at a meeting of Japanese managers and had them give talks about their suggestions.

The GI Club developed the Creative Idea Suggestion System and also functioned as a kind of home port for Watanabe's venture.

> *The suggestion manual put together by the GI Club was translated, and slowly but surely we began to see the types of ideas that had earned low-level prize money in Japan. But when we began to do things more thoroughly, there were some things our own strength and knowledge alone were not able to handle. I think we may have been slighting the section and division managers above us, but at such times we would dash off a fax to the GI Club and ask all the members to think about those things.*

When members involved in GI Club activities who did not know Watanabe saw the faxes he sent, they were impressed with the efforts he was making. But it was the understanding of his superiors and colleagues that played the most important role in establishing the Creative Idea Suggestion System at Mobilindo.

Managing director Onishi, the Creative Idea committee vice-chairman, had some doubts about the workplace and stopped by to visit Mobilindo. He contacted the Creative Idea committee secretariat and they considered various countermeasures. Those who made outstanding suggestions were given awards at Mobilindo also, but Onishi went out of his way to buy some dolls and bring them with him from Japan.

"You give out extra prizes, don't you?" he said to Watanabe. "Why don't you use these dolls for extra prizes?"

As Watanabe thought back about the time when he took up his assignment at Mobilindo, he said: "I saw the suggestion examples of workers at the workplace, but the number of suggestions was extremely small and the content amounted to simple descriptions of various phenomena. From our perspective there was material for suggestions all over the place, but not much was happening."

Tsuyoshi Bando put it this way:

Actually, when he was about to go to Indonesia, the GI Club had a wonderful send-off party for him. It may have been then that someone said something like, "Please popularize creative ideas over there too." But I never imagined that Watanabe, put in charge of one section as a manager and waving a flag at the workplace, would popularize creative ideas to such an extent.

Watanabe returned to Japan in the position of GI Club Chairman.

CHAPTER FOUR

"Grass-roots Power":
The Creative Ideas Behind
10 Outstanding Suggestions

Serious Problems Involving the Creative
Idea Suggestion System

By 1986, a cumulative total of 2,649,000 suggestions had been submitted at Toyota. Participation in the Creative Idea Suggestion System was 94 percent, with 47.7 suggestions per person per year.

However, the suggestion activities throughout the company were not without problems. Individuals varied widely in their commitment. As the Creative Idea committee secretariat put it, "If one person makes 1000 suggestions in a year, then another person is resigned to doing suggestions because he feels he has to. There were also variations between work areas. As Managing Director Onishi noted, "In maintenance and administrative divisions creative ideas are easy, and in assembly divisions they are difficult." Finally, there were a number of serious problems in the relationship between suggestion activities and the nature of a job.

The low quality of suggestions from the administrative divisions is a special problem. In the Toyota Creative Idea Suggestion System, the standard for an excellent idea is an idea for which the prize is ¥6000 ($45) or more. However, the fact that the standard is set at ¥4000 ($30) or more for the administrative divisions indicates the severe conditions involved.

If there were a ¥6000 hurdle in the administrative divisions where high-quality suggestions are difficult, the appeal, "Let's submit excellent suggestions!" would be reduced to mere formality, because the standard is too high to reach, so it is set lower to avoid a loss of spirit in suggestion activities. Koichi Masuda, a section manager in the Creative Idea committee executive office, says:

> Because the rules and methods of evaluation under the current system are derived from a production workplace orientation, there is no doubt that the same system is inappropriate for administration. In my opinion, I think a completely separate system for administration would be the best solution.

Masaki Oda of the public information bureau gave the following opinions on submitting suggestions in administration:

> In the production divisions, technical divisions, and so on, there are well-defined yardsticks for cutting time and reducing costs that are measurable in monetary terms, but the information activities I am in charge of are really services, and even if one talks about improving a service, it is difficult to convert increased service efficiency into time and costs. Consequently, the only way for assessing efficiency is to use my own judgment.

Suggestions are evaluated and graded by the assistant section managers and section managers, but as there are also no well-defined criteria for evaluation, such work is quite difficult.

Hisato Tomono, an assistant section manager in the general affairs department of the Tokyo branch office, illustrates the point:

> *For example, a suggestion came up saying, "To make a list, instead of writing 19 lines per page as we've done until now, we improved this to 20." How on earth am I supposed to evaluate this? This suggestion shouldn't even get the lowest award of ¥500 (less than $5); in practical terms it's very easy to total up lines this way. For something like this, the only thing possible is a sympathetic response of, "Well, let's give the ¥500." If a suggestion is at the ¥500 or ¥1000 level, we say, "That's great, let's do it." We don't give negative evaluations, only positive ones. We avoid being too harsh because there's always the threat of nipping suggestion activities in the bud.*

Using Suggestion Activities to Train People in Administrative Divisions

Creative Idea suggestion activities began in earnest at the Tokyo branch office of Toyota following a merger of manufacturing and sales in 1982. At the outset, suggestions focused on grievances or dissatisfaction with facilities such as "The light is dim" or "The elevator is slow."

As the employees began to understand creative ideas, their suggestions literally took the form of, "How about this?" Recently, at long last, suggestions submitted have matured to the point where there is complete implementation stating the benefits of the improvement and the problems resolved. Suggestions resulting in major improvements in office efficiency are definitely on the increase.

Administrative suggestions tend to reflect the time period. Currently, one-third of all suggestions concern office automation (OA), and they make up well over half in overseas offices. The other suggestions focus on things such as economizing on paper, reducing memo circulation, and decreasing inventory. Many of these receive evaluations only at the ¥500 level. According to Hisato Tomono:

> *Even in the case of excellent suggestions in the administrative divisions, when someone asks how much the company will benefit by paying a reward for such suggestions, the reward is generally higher than the benefits from work reductions, and there has actually been a loss of money.*
>
> *However, there may be one suggestion that will produce 100 million units in reduction efficiency. If all suggestions have been labeled worthless, suggestion activities will wither and excellent suggestions will not be made. Even if each suggestion does not produce a benefit above the cost of its award, it is important for Creative Idea suggestion activities to look at the overall picture and not just isolated incidents.*

Even the Creative Idea committee executive office does not seem to expect economic benefits from suggestions from the administrative divisions. As Koichi Masuda of the Creative Idea committee secretariat said:

> *The Japanese-style suggestion system differs from that of the United States in that there are expectations of increasing efficiency in general, not just economic efficiency. A system like the Creative Idea Suggestion System is also an important way to train people and make the workplace more dynamic. Therefore, even if the level of suggestions is low, rewards are given for them just as they are. The two roles – increasing economic efficiency and training people – cannot be ignored. Because work in an administrative division is service-oriented*

and because the Creative Idea Suggestion System nurtures an attitude among employees for doing work in a positive manner, it can be used to increase the quality of service, and thereby economic efficiency.

Tsuyoshi Bando, also of the secretariat, who has experience involving line operations, explained why high-quality suggestions simply do not come from the administrative divisions:

Because there are no standard operations in an office, it is harder to visualize improvements. On the other hand, where standard operations are the focus at the workplace, a target is raised and the number of units to be produced is clearly set. You can conclude that there is some problem if the target cannot be achieved. Consequently, you are usually in a position to easily detect problem points.

The problem of discerning the borderline between everyday work and creative ideas is also one of the special characteristics in the evaluation of suggestions from the administrative division. The evaluation method for the Toyota Creative Idea Suggestion System included a factor called the job duty demerit system. This is a method for reducing points when the suggestion submitted is within the range of one's immediate duties or makes an improvement in one's own work. In the case of suggestions by those in the position of assistant sections manager or higher, it is enforced unconditionally.

To illustrate with an extreme example, say a person in charge of purchasing submits as a suggestion, "As a result of price competition, it was possible to keep prices down." This is not a creative idea. It is simply part of the everyday work of the person who submitted it.

But the suggestion: "By *creating* competition among sellers when purchasing ball-point pens, it was possible to keep prices low." Here again, this is essentially the job of purchasing. However, the suggestion is on the borderline between fundamental duties and creative ideas. Because the situation is ambiguous, it is a troublesome aspect of suggestions in the administrative divisions.

Below are presented a number of suggestions submitted by Toyota employees. These illustrative suggestions include administrative suggestions in addition to excellent suggestions and standard level suggestions submitted from workplaces.

Studying Suggestion Examples: Outstanding Suggestions in Administrative Divisions

---

Example 1: Improving Methods for Overseas Remittances

Proponent: Ryoko Fujii
Collaborator: Keiji Kanazawa
Award: ¥15,000 ($1,153)

Point of the Example

Previously, a department handling something turned an overseas bill into a request for remittance. The request was distributed automatically by the business section of the overseas planning department, using a personal computer. However, making the request was complicated, and many people were involved in the process before remittance was sent.

This situation was a holdover from before the merger of the manufacturing and sales divisions. Although they were merged, the system for overseas remittance was not unified. As a result, the financial affairs department in Nagoya handled matters concerning the home office and the Nagoya branch office, while the accounting section of the Tokyo branch office informed the Nagoya financial affairs department of funding arrangements. Remittances forwarded from Nagoya were transferred to the bank.

The proponent, together with her collaborator in the financial affairs department, created a new remittance system, which unified remittance activities in the Nagoya financial affairs department and required only a single form for the remittance request.

Improvement Suggestion

A new remittance system like the one in Figure 4-1 was introduced.

The following points are worth noting:

- By standardizing the request form sent around from the departments to the financial affairs department and combining the remittance requests, the total can be used as remittance data.
- By changing the application forms sent to the bank to an in-house company form, the work can be handled by computer operations.
- The total can be sent directly to the accounting system of the accounting section.
- The totals can be used as remittance record data.

Benefits of the Improvement

Labor-hours saved:

- By unifying the various authorities concerned with remittances, it was possible to reduce labor-hours in the overseas planning department and the Tokyo accounting section.

- Labor-hours at the overseas planning department (input of remittance data, writing application reports, preparation of remittance tables and remittance slips,

Previous System

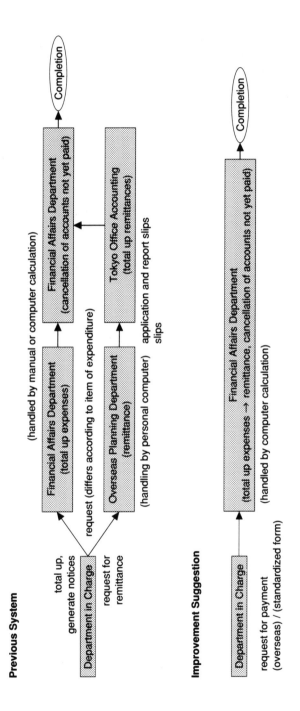

Improvement Suggestion

Figure 4-1.

tance slips, administration of records, payment of handling fees, acting as liaison with the bank, and so on) were reduced by 220 hours per month.

- Labor-hours in the Tokyo accounting section (handling cash flow, checking application forms, checking handling fee slips, acting as liaison with the bank, and so on) were reduced by 20 hours per month.
- Labor-hours in a department (coding the remittee, and so on) were reduced by 10 hours per month.

- Paper reduction.

  - The number of forms was reduced by 400 sets per month.
  - Preparation of remittance related documents – 750 pages per month – in the overseas planning department was eliminated.
  - 250 pages per month were eliminated in the Tokyo accounting section.

- Improvement of the work system.

  - The totaling of payments in arrears and their cancellations was systematized in the Nagoya financial affairs department.
  - There was no longer a need for a liaison from the overseas planning office and the Tokyo accounting office to the Nagoya financial affairs department, and there a reduction was made in labor-hours for checking.
  - The way is paved for a smooth transition to electronic requests in the future.

- Standardized records make the process in the department go smoothly.

Investments Necessary for Improvements

- Labor-hours were increased by 40 per month in the financial affairs department.
- Development costs of ¥260,000 ($2000) per month were required in the computer operations department.

Example 2: Improving Reception System for Ochanomizu Dormitories

Proponent: Yumi Toyama
Award: ¥4000 ($30)

Point of the Example

The personnel section of the headquarters office was in charge of the Ochanomizu dormitory registration and reception. That department was connected by facsimile and telephone with the personnel section in Tokyo, and the Tokyo personnel section in turn was connected by mail or telephone with the Ochanomizu dormitory. While such an arrangement would seem to present no particular problems, in practice when there was a sudden change or a sudden request for a room, troubles appeared one after another.

The question was asked, "Is it really sensible to go through the personnel department of the head office?" Consequently, a facsimile machine was introduced at the Ochanomizu dormitory, and reception activities were centralized in the Tokyo personnel section.

Improvement Suggestion

- Having the registration and reception activities that had been performed by the personnel section in the headquarters office transferred to the personnel section in Tokyo reduced the duplication in labor-hours within the company.

- The personnel section in Tokyo received new duties but took measures to reduce labor-hours as much as possible.
  - The reception register was changed.
  - The employee's title and position were written in a simple phonetic alphabet for clear communication by telephone with the Tokyo personnel section.
  - Installation of a facsimile machine at the Ochanomizu dormitory reduced the labor-hours necessary for communicating with the dormitory and also prevented mistakes from occurring.
  - All the personnel in charge of Benefits Subsection 2 handle reception.

Benefits of the Improvement

- The labor-hours required for reception activities were reduced from 1772 minutes (29 hours, 32 minutes) per month to 680 minutes (11 hours, 20 minutes) per month, and a transfer of control in activities was accomplished.
- Accommodation of people requesting rooms has become smooth, and service has become better.
- Because fewer people are involved in confirmation, cancellations are handled quickly and reliably.

Investment Needed for Improvement

Facsimile installation costs (¥2083 ($16) per month for leasing, ¥2350 ($18) per month for basic rate).

Example 3: Improving Methods to Collect Fees for Self-study English Conversation Courses

Proponent: Akiko Kamiya
Collaborators: Miki Kawashima, Naoko Sasaki, Fumiko Morinaga
Award: ¥4000 ($30)

Point of the Example

At Toyota, when there is a recognized need for employees to take English conversation courses for business reasons, the company bears the total cost. To encourage employees who wish to study English on their own, the company bears half the cost of the course.

In a half-year course taken by 80 people, each employee brought his or her ¥15,000 ($115) course fee to the personnel section separately. The personnel section, however, could not transfer the money to the accounting section until it had collected the full ¥1.2 million ($9200). Consequently, some risk was involved administratively, and there was waste because the cash remained idle during that time.

Improvement Suggestion

An account was opened with Mitsui Bank on the seventh floor of the Tokyo branch office exclusively for English conversation course fees, and people taking a course paid their fee directly to the bank.

The previous fee collection system and the system after improvement are shown in Figure 4-2.

Benefits of the Improvement

- Total labor-hours for collection of course fees was reduced 95 percent, from 540 minutes to 30 minutes.
- The number of delinquent payers dropped from 25 people per course to none.
- The followup work for delinquent payers dropped 100 percent from 50 minutes to 0 minutes.
- There was no longer any need to manage a safe-deposit box.
- The time needed for the paperwork involved in depositing money in the accounting section dropped from 30 minutes to 0 minutes.

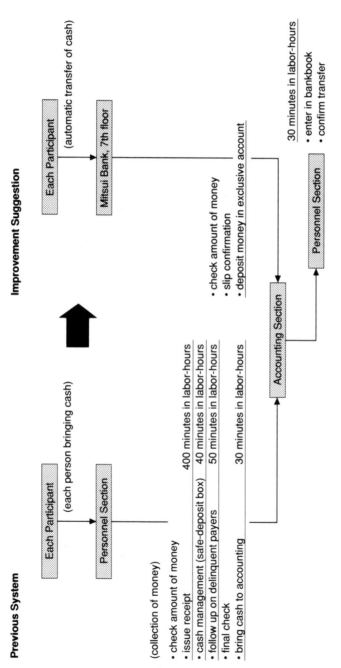

Figure 4-2.

- Labor-hours in the accounting section dropped from 30 minutes to 0 minutes.
  Total reduction in labor-hours: from 650 minutes to 30 minutes.
- As an additional benefit, improvement can be planned in examination fee collection for English examinations in the company.

Example 4: Faster Issuing of Overseas Sales Reports

Proponent: Kazuko Fukuda
Award: ¥6000 ($45)

Point of the Example

The overseas sales report is the single in-house publication that shows the overall business performance of the divisions on a monthly basis. It is seen even by top management. Around the 10th of each month, each department would prepare a handwritten manuscript, and the section of the department assigned to do so checked words and phrases, expressions, and figures and put it together. The manuscript was then sent to the typing room, checked again, and then printed and sent out.

Even though the manuscript was received on the 10th, the finished version was not sent out until after the 20th. Ways to speed up preparation of the report had been sought for a long time. Accordingly, a solution was found for improving work efficiency by using word processors.

Improvement Suggestion

- Each department, including the section designated to double check the manuscript, switched from preparing a handwritten copy to using a word processor for preparing the manuscript.
  - For entries common to each department, the designated section prepares a standard blank form on a

floppy disk, and each department simply keys in the numbers.
- For entries needing an explanation, each department can make entries by word processor in the entry summary prepared by the designated section.
- After a simple check of the word processed manuscripts submitted by each department, they are immediately sent to printing.

Benefits of the Improvement
- The report was sent out faster: from after the 20th of each month to around the 15th of each month.
- Labor-hours in the typing room were reduced from 15 labor-hours per month to 0.
- Labor-hours for checking were reduced from 15 labor-hours per month to 3 labor-hours.
- Because the departments simply shifted the time consumed by checking handwritten copies to word processing operations, there was no added cost.

Studying Suggestion Examples: Outstanding Suggestions in Technical Divisions

Example 5: Idea for Load Device to Be Used in Testing Strength of Rear Seat Backs

Proponent: Osamu Miura

Point of the Example

The safety experiment section of the Number 2 Vehicle Experiment Division is mainly engaged in testing to investigate and develop safety performance for parts in the interiors of automobiles. One of these tests is to investigate whether the back seat of the car is strong enough to stay intact when the vehicle suffers a rear end collision.

In the test exactly the same load has to impact at the same time on each seat back of a three-person seat. It took a long time to reach the target load, and it was difficult to get the loads for all three seats uniform. This idea is an example of utilizing the pulley principle to solve these problems in one stroke.

Conditions Before Improvement

In the previous test method, one wire was attached to the left and right seats, while a separate wire was attached to the middle seat. Two people used a chain block from behind to pull. The two workers watched the wave patterns on a measuring device and adjusted the loads while signaling each other. This method had the following problems (see Figure 4-3):

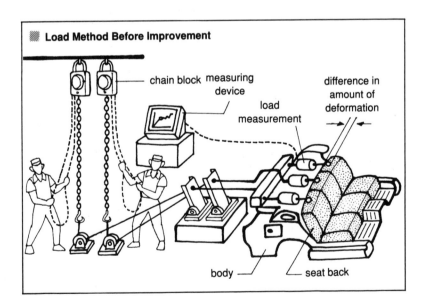

Figure 4-3.

1. Because the amount of deformation of the load points for the left and right seats and the middle seat differed, if one side was pulled up, the other went down, creating a load imbalance. Keeping the loads the same was very difficult even for experienced workers.
2. Considerable time was needed to take the load to the target value with this method.

Improvement Suggestion

Taking a hint from the principle of the equilibrium of forces based on wires and pulleys, a way of answering these problems was refined so that the same loads impacted the three points simultaneously, keeping the load variance within a few percent. Only one person was needed to do the work.

First a device that combined seven pulleys and wires was tried. (See Figure 4-4.) However, because the wiring was fixed at the ends in this method, the rolling resistance of the seven pulleys was built up between the left and right seats. When the resistance became great, a considerable load variance remained if a difference was created in the amount of deformation between the left and right seats.

After lengthy study of this first device, two more pulleys were added, and the fixed-end system was changed to an endless system. With this system, there are only four pulleys in between the left and right seats, and the load variance from friction is lowered a few percent.

Benefits of the Improvement

- Load precision improved.
  - The greatest load variance between the seats was greatly reduced.
  - It is possible to get a reliable load in a short time.
- One worker was needed instead of two, and labor-hours were reduced.

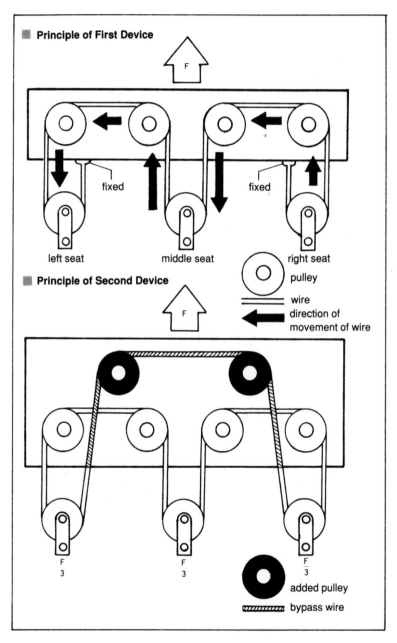

Figure 4-4.

- The operations were simple enough for anyone to perform – expertise was no longer necessary.

Example 6: Idea for Belt Pump

Proponent: Koichi Hatayama
Collaborator: Jun Matsuda

Point of the Example

At the Kamigo plant, machine tools for processing transmission gears occupy over half of the plant space. The oil for cutting and shaving that collected in the oil pans of these machine tools was removed by pumps, but when chips and dust clogged the pumps, they would suddenly cease to function. This was a chronic occurrence.

Conditions Before Improvement

At the workplace, various processes were tried when pumps clogged up, but with no success; inevitably workers had to scoop out the oil by hand. Consequently, a pump that used a cloth belt and was based on a completely different concept was made.

Improvement Suggestion

A pump like the one in Figure 4-5 was devised that scooped up oil in a way completely different from that of the impeller and rotor system pumps being used in the plant. The idea was suggested by the wringing out of a scrubbing cloth. Standard household carpet material is used for the belt. The oil easily soaks into it, and it is difficult for chips and sludge to clog it.

Tests were conducted to determine how much time was needed for this device to scoop up 20 liters of oil with different speed reduction ratios in the motor. The test results showed that 5 1/2 hours were needed for speed reducers (4GK-180K)

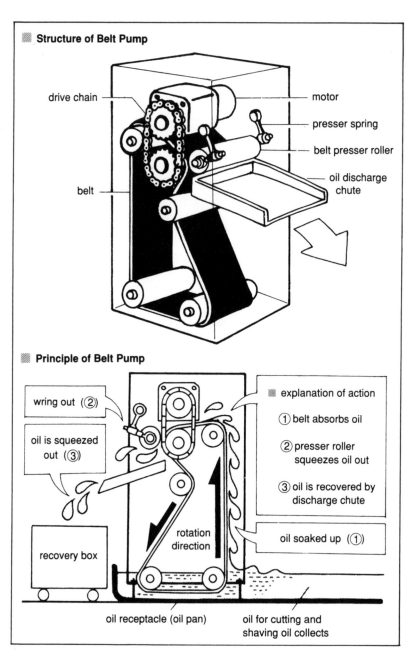

Figure 4-5.

Factors \ Type	Coolant Pump	Trochoid Pump	Fluid Pump	Belt Pump
Air (strong suction)	×	○	◎	◎
Chips (strong suction)	×	×	×	◎
Sludge (strong suction)	×	×	×	◎
Durability	○	◎	○	◎
Picks up small quantities	×	○	△	◎
Easy to transport	△	△	○	◎
Amount of discharge	◎	◎	○	○

◎ = excellent
○ = good
△ = average
× = poor

Figure 4-6. Comparison of Pump Performances

with large gear ratios. However, with 4GK-50K-type speed reducers, which were used in the second test, scooping up time was reduced to one hour. In addition, for small gear ratios with a fast rotational speed, a scoop-up time of 10 minutes was achieved by a finished product using a 5GK-5K type.

Benefits of the Improvement

A performance comparison of three types of pumps is given in Figure 4-6. As is clear by looking at Figure 4-6, even the absorption of chips and sludge or cotton dust has no effect, and workers no longer have to scoop by hand.

———————————

Example 7: Idea for Method of Affixing Vertical Saw Disc Wheel Rubber

Proponent: Yuji Hashiguchi

Point of the Example

In the aftertreatment process of the aluminum foundry line, a vertical saw is used for cutting the separating block for each type of foundry item. (See Figure 4-7.) The blade of this saw is turned by a drive wheel, and on the wheel a rubber ring is affixed with a bonding agent to prevent the saw blade from slipping. When the rubber ring wore out, changing it required many labor-hours, and the work had an extremely low level of efficiency. The idea in this example suggested a slip prevention measure that used no bonding agents and was easily changed.

Conditions Before Improvement

The previous method by which the rubber ring was installed on the wheel is as shown in Figure 4-7.

After removing the wheel from the saw disc and washing off the clinging dust, a bonding agent was applied to both the wheel and a rubber ring, and they were fastened in place. This method created the following problems:

- Liquid coolant, which is used in cutting aluminum foundry items, sticks on the wheel, making the rubber swell and come off.
- Although the wheel and rubber are fastened with a bonding agent, the bonding strength is not adequate, and separation is easy.
- Dust from cutting adheres to the rubber, shortening its lifetime.

Improvement Suggestion

A method was devised in which a part of the wheel was altered, using a timing belt rather than the rubber ring to prevent slipping. (See Figure 4-8).

Initially, one place was cut out in the timing belt, and both its ends were fastened to the wheel. This method had the following characteristics:

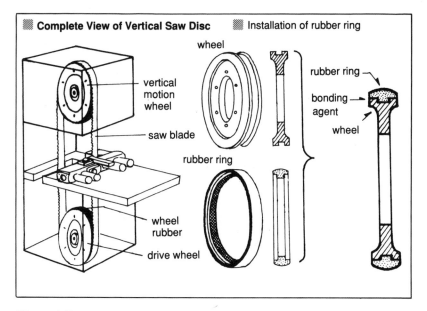

Figure 4-7.

- *Length adjustment of the timing belt:* The timing belt is put through the inlet hole of the wheel, cut to an appropriate length, and two installation holes are opened for fastening fittings.
- *Setting the belt in the wheel:* The timing belt, which is put into the wheel, is fastened to fitting A with two bolts, and fitting B is installed in the wheel.
- *Fastening:* Rotating fitting C has a pulling effect so as to change the spacing between fittings A and B, and the belt is securely fastened to the wheel.

However, this method causes the following problems:

- Cutting the timing belt and making adjustments for the appropriate length takes time.

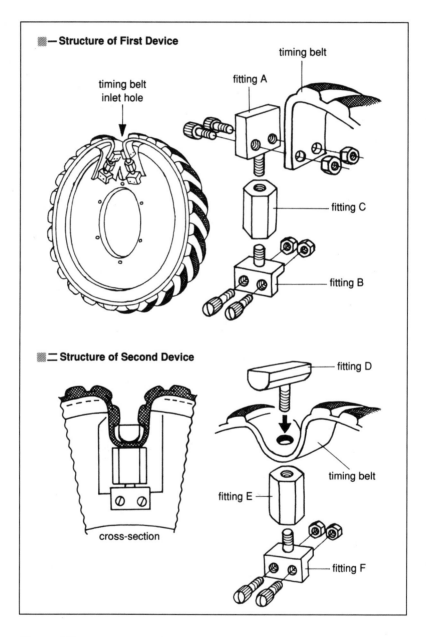

Figure 4-8.

- If one pulls too hard, the belt at the hole for fitting A will be torn off.

Consequently, another method was devised as shown in Figure 4-8. The timing belt is not cut, and only one hole is opened. Fitting D is passed through the hole and connected to fitting E. Next, by fastening fitting F to the wheel with two bolts, everything is set in place.

When the distance of D and F is regulated by turning E, tension is applied, and the timing belt is tightly fastened to the wheel by its own tension.

Benefits of the Improvement

- It became easy to change the slip prevention device.
- Because the timing belt can be fastened more tightly than with bonding agents, the slip prevention device no longer comes off.
- An inexpensive timing belt could be used to prevent slipping.

Example 8: Idea and Application for a Towed Tractor Inertia Braking Device

Proponent: Osamu Gotoh
Collaborator: Seigo Miyashita

The transportation section of the Number 3 Technical Department adopted a transport method of linked tractors to transport parts to each office in the technical division. However, there was a problem of insufficient braking power with this coupled transport; smooth stopping was not possible.

This suggestion found an answer to the safety problem by taking a hint from the movement of a pendulum.

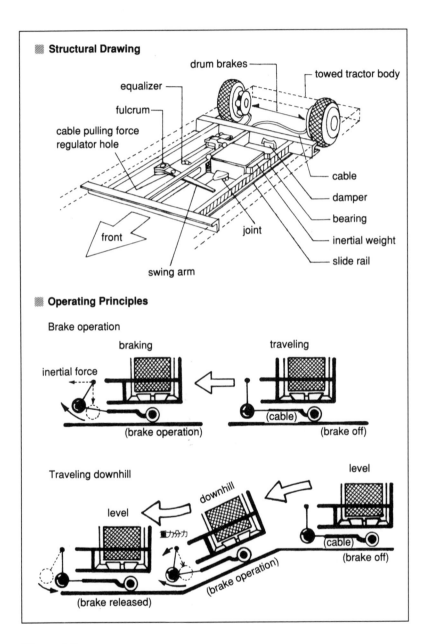

Figure 4-9.

Conditions Before Improvement

The previous method of transport had the following problems:

- The tractors were equipped with brakes only on the rear wheels, and when the brakes were applied for sudden stops, the tractor was pushed from behind by the towed tractors, making a smooth stop impossible. In addition, the towed tractors would twist and turn when going downhill.
- To ensure safety, traveling speed was held down as much as possible (five to seven kilometers per hour), which lowered transport efficiency.

Improvement Suggestion

By applying the concept of the movement of a pendulum weight, a system was devised in which the brake is applied by the force of gravity going downhill. On a level road, once the brake is applied, inertial force releases it naturally.

As shown in Figure 4-9, the device consists of a slide rail, inertial weight, swing arm, equalizer, drum brakes, and cable. This arrangement transmits the movement of the inertial weight to the brakes.

Explanation of the working system

- When the brake is applied the inertial weight moves forward over the slide rail.
- A joint in the front part of the inertial weight pushes the swing arm.
- The equalizer is pulled forward by the movement of the swing arm.
- The drum brakes function through the cable connected to the equalizer, and the braking power is applied.
- When speed reduction ceases on a level road, the force

of the inertial weight pushing the swing arm ceases, and the braking power is automatically released.

Special features of the system

- Based on the angle of the downhill slope and the rate of speed reduction and so on, the appropriate braking power is obtained, and driving can be done with a greater degree of safety.
- By changing the inertial weight and the swing arm, the appropriate braking power can be obtained for a variety of towed tractors.
- Few parts are needed for the system, its arrangement and installation are simple, and it is highly reliable.

Benefits of the Improvement

- Braking power increased, braking distance was cut in half. The twisting and turning when going downhill also ceased.
- The cargo load capacity that allows a safe braking distance was approximately doubled.
- There was no longer a need to travel at the slowest possible speed, and efficiency in transport was achieved.

Example 9: Reducing Transportation Costs by Decreasing the Size of Boxes for Corolla Knock-down Sets Going to Indonesia

Proponent: Ryoji Mori
Collaborator: Noboru Ogata

Point of the Example

The parts section has two major functions in its work. One is shipping to domestic body and assembly plants vehicle structural parts such as the fuel tanks, bumpers, and sheets that form the framework of the automobile. The other is collection and packing of domestic and foreign manufactured parts, and shipping them knocked-down (CKD) to Toyota manufacturing plants in 10 overseas countries such as the United States (NUMMI), Kenya, Thailand, Indonesia, Australia, and Venezuela.

In CKD, automobile parts are exported to a partner country where complete automobiles are put together at assembly plants. The state of subassembly varies with the technological level of production in the partner country.

According to a study by the number 2 packing and transportation committee at Toyota, roughly speaking, over half the cost of such work is due to transportation costs. To take Indonesia, for example, which has the most shipments, the amount was as much as ¥28 million ($215,384) a year just for transporting the floor case of one type of sedan handled by the Takaoka plant.

This suggestion involves changing the wooden boxes used to ship CKD to improve transportation costs.

Conditions Before Improvement

As shown in Figure 4-10, previous wooden boxes were made from a combination of wood and veneer panels. The external dimensions were determined by the size of the parts and the thickness of the partition panels. The minimum width required of the panels was 51 millimeters to maintain strength, and a reduction in the overall size of a wooden box could only come with a design change in the part.

In addition, because the wood was joined by riveting machines, the safety aspect of the work also presented problems.

Improvement Suggestion

It is possible to reduce the size of the wooden box by changing the material of the partition panels. Except for portions where wood was absolutely necessary, 5 partition panels

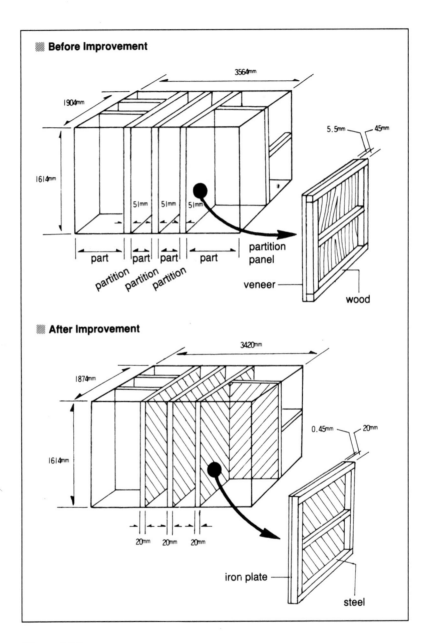

Before Improvement

3564mm

1904mm

1614mm

51mm 51mm 51mm

5.5mm   45mm

part part part part part

partition partition partition

partition panel

veneer

wood

After Improvement

3420mm

1874mm

1614mm

20mm 20mm 20mm

0.45mm   20mm

iron plate

steel

Figure 4-10.

of 51 millimeter width were changed from wood to steel plates. Because strength was reinforced with steel at a thickness of 20.5 millimeters, the length of the box could be reduced by 144 millimeters, and the width by 30 millimeters. The overall volume was reduced by 0.593m³.

Benefits of the Improvement

- Transportation costs were reduced by ¥563,000 ($4330) per year (¥143/vehicle × 340 vehicles/month × 12).
- Labor-hours were reduced, with a total cost reduction of ¥600,000 ($4615) per year (¥50,000/month× 12).
  - Reduction in labor-hours by decreasing time needed for hammering was 11 hours per month.
  - Using a hoist for packaging, rather than two people as previously, reduced labor-hours 3.4 hours per month.
- Safety was increased by the decrease in the number of times for hammering (47 times per case).
- Positioning the partition panels has become simple, and unsatisfactory assembly has disappeared.
- Packing and transfer operations at the export destination have become easy, and partition panels can be reused for pallets and other things.
- In the future, lateral development for other cases such as body cases is possible.

Total benefit: ¥30 million ($230,769) per year.

Example 10: Shortening Operations for Changing Drills
Proponent: Hidetoshi Ohbuchi

Point of the Example

One operation of the machinery department is processing propeller shafts that send the driving force of the engine to the wheels. The drill process of the flange companion that is used in the coupling part of the propeller shaft involves different diameter holes according to the vehicle type and requires changing drills, which was causing work delays.

The suggestion succeeded in making the operation efficient by changing the shape of the drill.

Conditions Before Improvement

There are four types of drill blades, 11.3 ϕ, 10.3 ϕ, 9.3 ϕ, and 8.3 ϕ, which are used according to the part being processed. The times for changing vehicle types, done according to the sign boards within the stages of work, involve two shifts with three changes per shift per day, meaning a total of six changing operations were required each day.

Approximately 2 minutes are needed for one drill change. However, the problem is that when the drill blade is changed, the drill bushing (see Figure 4-11) also has to be changed, and that requires another 10 minutes. If work is done without using a bushing, the drill will crack, the hole will become an oval, the positioning will be off, and various other abnormalities will result. In the end, 12 minutes were taken up by the change operation.

Improvement Suggestion

The solution to reducing the number of labor-hours for the change operation lies in being able to use all four types of blades with one bushing. Consequently, the following things became clear as a result of numerous experiments.

- The bushing aperture is 11.3 ϕ. However, the length of the bushing must be 20 mm.
- A blade edge of 7.5 mm is sufficient for making holes.

A step drill, which satisfied the condition in (2) of being able to make the four types of holes, was devised, together

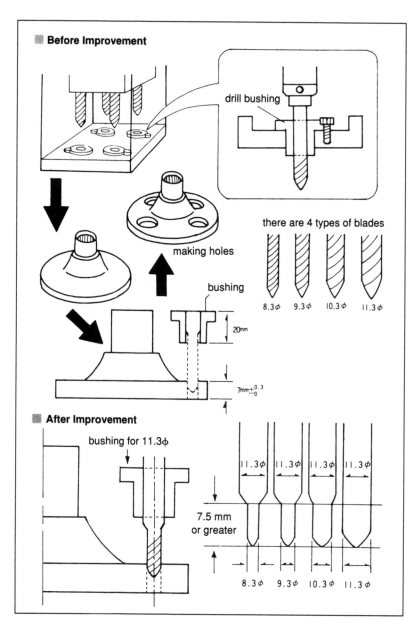

Figure 4-11.

with the use of the bushing in (1). Whenever any hole is being made with this method, no gap is created between the drill blade and the bushing, so the hole can be made.

Benefits of the Improvement

- A reduction in labor-hours of 11 hours per day was achieved. (10 minutes (for changing the bushing) × 2 (reset) × 3 times per shift (number of changes) × 2 shifts). [set multiplication symbols]
- Because there were no more delays in the change operation, later stages of work were not adversely affected.
- Safety increased, and the tool storage area was reduced.

———

CHAPTER FIVE

"Toyotaism:" The Fundamental Precepts That Brought About the Creative Idea Suggestion System

The Driving Force Behind Toyota's High Profits

Every person at the workplace freely and enthusiastically accepts the challenges involved in reducing costs and building a better workplace environment. What is the real source of this energy, visible throughout the entire company in Toyota's Creative Idea suggestion activities? As a reporter on economics for many years, I was responsible for covering the automotive industry. During those years I kept wondering just what kind of a company Toyota Motor Company was. Indeed, many books have been written about Toyota, one of the leading companies in the industrial world and perhaps the most typical Japanese company. It is only natural for those who write economic journals to pay attention to Toyota.

Interest in the company became even more intense when Toyota was able to boast high profits after the Japanese economy moved into a low-growth period because of the oil crises in 1973 and 1979. One of the driving forces behind such high profits was Toyota's unique production system, sometimes called the "*kanban* system" because it uses kanban (production order cards). This term has become widely known not only in Japan, but throughout the world.

In *The Toyota Production System*, the late Taiichi Ohno, former vice president of Toyota Motor Company and father of the kanban system, states that the Toyota production system is based on two major components: "just-in-time" and "autonomation."*

The term "just-in-time" is used to denote a situation in which the parts required for assembly arrive at the production line only when they are needed, and only in the quantities required. The expression "just-in-time" is a Japanese-English phrase coined by the founder of Toyota Motor Company, Kiichirō Toyoda. The Japanese words for "on time" or "on schedule" are equivalent to the English phrase, "just on time." Kiichirō's phrase, just-in-time, was based on the idea that only the necessary amount of what was required should be produced each day. Implementing just-in-time means that the job can be done without keeping things in stock. From the perspective of production control, this is an ideal situation. However, automobiles are assembled with about 20,000 parts, so an enormous number of processing operations is required. With so many processes it is not so easy to maintain a just-in-time situation without slip-ups in production planning. There are many factors that require changes in production planning: inaccurate estimates, administrative errors, defects and rework, equipment break-

---

* The late Taiichi Ohno's *Toyota Production System* and two other books are published in English by Productivity Press. See also Japan Management Association's *Kanban: Just-In-Time at Toyota* (Productivity Press, 1989, edited by David Lu) and Shigeo Shingo, *A Study of the Toyota Production System from an Industrial Engineering Perspective* (Productivity Press, 1989) for more information about the Toyota production system. – Ed.

The late Taiichi Ohno, former vice president of Toyota Motor Company and vice-chairman of the Creative Idea Suggestion Committee.

downs. When a process has a problem, there will be a shortage of parts needed by a subsequent process, and the production plan will have to change, possibly causing line stops.

If these kinds of situations are simply ignored and production planning done independently by each process, there will be a shortage of required parts. On the other hand, there will also be cases when parts not needed right away will stack up sky-high. While this may seem only natural, these situations result in additional problems, such as the inability to distinguish between normal and abnormal at the assembly lines of each production site. When there is a delay in correcting an abnormality, too many workers will make too many parts. Ohno therefore concluded that "to produce using just-in-time so that each process receives the exact item needed, when it is needed, and in the quantity needed, conventional management methods do not work well."*

---

* Ohno, op. cit., at 4.

Just-In-Time and Autonomation

Just-in-time provided an ideal situation for production control because work could be done without stockpiling. Ohno gave the following explanation of his idea: "I kept thinking about how to supply the number of parts needed just-in-time. The flow of production is the transfer of materials. So, I tried thinking about the transport of materials in the reverse direction."*

Conventional thinking has the previous process supplying things to the subsequent process. In the case of automobiles, materials are processed and made into parts. Parts are then assembled and made into unit parts and then sent to the final assembly line. But Ohno thought about reversing this flow. Instead of the work flow going from a previous process to a subsequent process, it would go from a subsequent process to a previous process. He created a situation in which only the amount needed was taken at the time it was needed. So he used kanban, or order production cards, as a method of linking each process by indicating only how much of any item was needed. The amounts required were controlled by kanban. This was indeed a case of "reverse thinking."

As discussed in chapter 1, Ohno went to the United States in 1956 to observe Ford factories. At that time he was also keenly interested in supermarkets, which were not yet very common in Japan. Things sold in supermarkets are bought by customers only when they are needed and only in the amounts needed. Cash registers are used for the things purchased and records are made. Supermarkets function as stores that continually replenish things.

Ohno thought about how this kind of arrangement could be applied to automobile production processes. If the previ-

---

* Ohno, op. cit., at 5.

ous process functioned as the supermarket and the subsequent process functioned as the customer, then it would also be possible for automobile production processes to have a just-in-time supply system in which whatever is needed would be supplied only when it is needed and only in the amounts needed.

Production plans are shown to the assembly line, with the starting point as the general assembly line, the final part of the manufacturing processes. People working on a subsequent process go to people working on a previous process to get parts needed on the assembly line: whatever is needed, whenever it is needed, and only the amount that is needed. People in the previous process produce only what people in the subsequent process need to replace.

When this system is implemented, movement goes upstream from the manufacturing processes to materials processing divisions, making it possible to link things together with a single thread. The kanban cards are used to indicate the giving and taking of things between processes as well as precisely how many things are desired. The kanban system is a means of making the two pillars of the Toyota production system – just-in-time and autonomation – function smoothly.

Autonomation is the second fundamental component of the Toyota production system. The Japanese characters for "automation" are pronounced "jidohka," which means "self-moving." At Toyota, they are also pronounced "jidohka," but the middle character, "doh," is *written* as the character for "work" instead of the character for "move." This changes the meaning to something like "self-working." *

---

* In English, this distinction is often expressed by referring to Toyota's term as "autonomation," or "automation with a human touch."— Ed.

There is a definite reason for this distinction. A machine operates when a human being presses a switch. But when some abnormality occurs, damage may result from the auto- matic mass-production of defective goods. Toyota uses the word *jidohka* – automation – for situations in which human beings just press switches to operate machines that cannot be checked automatically for malfunctions and that cannot be stopped from mass-producing defective goods.

On the other hand, the word *jidohka* – autonomation – is used for situations in which machines are equipped with mechanisms to make them stop automatically when some abnormality occurs – in other words, machines that have had a kind of human knowledge installed in them. In an autono- mation situation, human beings do nothing when machines are functioning normally. Only if the machine stops because of some abnormality do they need to interfere. One individu- al, therefore, can be in charge of many machines, and this naturally results in the improvement of productive efficiency.

This concept of autonomation was first developed by Sakichi Toyoda for the automatic loom he invented. The auto- matic loom senses when a warp or weft thread breaks and shuts down immediately to avoid producing defective goods.

Autonomation, which means that the machine stops oper- ating whenever there is some abnormality, depends on clearly identifying the cause of any abnormality that occurs. If the cause is clearly known, improvements can be made. For every abnormality that occurs, Toyota has its workers ask "why?" five times. When a machine stops operating, this pro- cess is put into action. The first thing to do is to consider why the machine has stopped. It becomes clear that a fuse blew because of an overload. The next thing to do is to search for the reason for the overload. It then becomes clear that there was not enough lubrication for the bearings.

Why wasn't there enough lubrication? The pump was not pumping up enough lubricant. The question of why enough lubricant was not being pumped up is then investigated, and it becomes clear that the pump shaft was vibrating as a result of abrasion. The fifth "why" is asked – what caused this abrasion? Because there was no filter, chips of the material had gotten in. A filter is therefore installed in the machine to ensure that the same problem will not occur again.

When abnormalities occur, the best way to deal with the situation is to ask "why?" five times so that the basic causes of the abnormalities can be investigated. Obviously, the same trouble will occur again if the investigation is not thorough. Autonomation means that when an abnormality occurs, it is possible to investigate its basic causes. And this also means that the employees working there will improve their performance.

A Fundamental Toyota Concept: Thorough Elimination of Waste

Ohno compared the relationship between just-in-time and autonomation, to baseball:

Autonomation corresponds to the skill and talent of individual players while just-in-time is the teamwork involved in reaching an agreed-upon objective.

For example, a player in the outfield has nothing to do as long as the pitcher has no problems. But a problem – the opposing batter getting a hit, for example – activates the outfielder who catches the ball and throws it to the baseman "just in time" to put the runner out.

Managers and supervisors in a manufacturing plant are like the team manager and the batting, base, and field coaches. A strong baseball team has mastered the plays; the players can meet any situation with coordinated action. In manufacturing, the production team that has mastered the just-in-time system is exactly like a baseball team that plays well together.

Autonomation, on the other hand, performs a dual role. It eliminates overproduction, an important waste in manufacturing, and prevents the production of defective products. To accomplish this, standard work procedures, corresponding to each player's ability, must be adhered to at all times. When abnormalities arise – that is, when a player's ability cannot be brought out – special instruction must be given to bring the player back to normal. This is an important duty of the coach.

In the autonomated system, visual control, or "management by sight," can help bring production weaknesses (in each player, that is) to the surface. This allows us then to take measures to strengthen the players involved.*

The Toyota production system is based on the idea that waste must be completely eliminated. Sakichi Toyoda developed his first autonomated machines with just that in mind – that defective goods, a form of waste, should not be created. The effort to eliminate waste, then, has been a fundamental concept of the Toyota Group since its early days.

The following kinds of waste are watched closely at Toyota production sites:

- Waste from overproduction.
- Waste from too much stock on hand.
- Transportation waste.
- Waste in the process itself.
- Inventory waste.

---

* Ohno, op. cit., at 7-8.

- Waste in operations.
- Waste from defects.

At Toyota, even waste in design is considered. Automobile models are changed every four to six years, and at that time the design is completely changed and the latest technology is introduced. Manufacturing methods are also changed, and production equipment is replaced with equipment that has adopted the latest technology. Detailed studies are made from the perspectives of performance, quality, and cost so that a better product can be offered to customers.

Automobiles, however, are composed of an enormous number of parts. All of these parts are not necessarily manufactured and designed without waste. Toyota, therefore, conducts value engineering (VE) and value analysis (VA) activities as ways of eliminating waste in design and manufacturing methods. VE involves activities designed to reduce costs by analyzing value before mass production. VA involves activities designed to reduce costs by analyzing values for products and drawings after mass production has begun. The focus in VA is on project teams, composed of workers from many divisions, such as the design technology division, the production technology division, production site workers, parts makers, and so on.

There is a famous story about cost reduction, involving a campaign to reduce the cost of Corollas. The Corolla is the most mass-produced car in the world. That fact alone means that any benefit resulting from cost reduction will be significant. The original goal was to cut costs by ¥10,000 ($75) per unit, but the actual cost reduction was ¥12,000 ($92). Consequently, savings for the Corolla alone amounted to about ¥10 billion ($75 million) a year. The idea of eliminating waste, permeating every nook and cranny within the company, is an intrinsic element of the Toyota way.

Toyota City: A Company Town

Another reason the Toyota production system became possible was the geographic proximity of its own factory clusters and its cooperating suppliers' plants.

The first thing one sees when one exits the Tomei Expressway at the Toyota Interchange is a banner strung across the street that reads: "WELCOME TO TOYOTA CITY." It is a medium-sized city, with a population of 300,000, about 40 minutes from the Japan National Railways Nagoya Station. Driving another 10 minutes, one arrives at Toyota headquarters, a four-story building made of reinforced concrete. With this building in the center, eleven factory clusters are concentrated within Toyota City, boasting a very spacious site with a total area of about 7,160,000 square kilometers. The

Toyota Headquarters

main factory, the one that is nearest the headquarters building, occupies 790,000 square meters, with a building area of 420,000 square meters. Nine other factories are situated around the headquarters and the main factory, and two others are located farther from headquarters.

When you drive around Toyota City, you notice here and there the signs of factories that cooperate with Toyota. The main factory, factory clusters, and cooperating factories turn Toyota City into a small Toyota kingdom. (On the top floor of the hotel where I stayed there was a restaurant called "Crown.") The whole town belongs to Toyota and it goes without saying that this made introducing the Toyota production system much easier.

The Toyota production system reached maturity during a period when Taiicho Ohno's authority was expanding. It was in 1950, while Ohno was the director of the Koromo machine factory that he began coping with the problems of the Toyota production system. He was responsible for rearranging the machines for just-in-time production, a kind of defensive area. Whenever the defensive area expanded, the Toyota production system had to be organized within that area. The system was eventually introduced throughout the entire company, including the supplier factories that cooperated with Toyota. There were quite a few factory clusters concentrated in Toyota City, and the cooperating factories were expanding around them. Their geographical proximity were a major reason why the Toyota production system could be introduced to the cooperating factories as well. They also played a major role in the thorough implanting of Toyota's fundamental concept of waste elimination.

In this manner, the Toyota production system gained a position of special authority after the oil crisis of 1973. This pushed Toyota to the forefront as a company representing Japan to the world.

An Essential Relationship of Mutual Trust

Before just-in-time production was developed, the flow of production caused the body of a car to be made by moving from one process to a subsequent process in a "push" system. Control of production flow was then reversed so that the subsequent process would go back to the previous process and take only the parts that were required, only when they were required, and only in the amount required. A kanban, or production card, was moved from a subsequent process to a previous process, thereby controlling the required production amounts in a "pull" system. This idea of "just-in-time" was one of the major components of the Toyota production system, aiming at the elimination of waste.

For this system to work, each process has to have a sense of trust built into it. This feeling comes from knowing that the production volume of parts is exactly what is indicated on the kanban, and that the parts will be supplied at the times indicated. The Toyota production system is built on this sense of mutual trust and a belief that people try inherently to accommodate the needs of others.

Without this sense of trust, the system would not work. The people who deal with materials processing might do more materials processing than the kanban calls for, "just in case," and still deliver to the next process only the production amount indicated. This would lead right back to wasteful stacks of work-in-process. Another aspect of the mutual trust at Toyota is that bad work is just not sent to the next process. If an employee neglects to deal with abnormal operations and then sends work to the next process, the automobile that results will be defective and the company will incur a loss. In this system each employee has the right to stop the entire production line. This also requires trust and confidence that the line will not be stopped unless there is some process abnormality.

The idea behind autonomation is to eliminate the wasteful mass production of defective items by having machines shut down automatically whenever abnormalities occur. This idea is also adopted for factories with people working on the assembly lines. When a production worker is likely to fall behind in the work he or she is responsible for, or detects some quality defect, he or she pulls a nearby switch that lights up a yellow lamp with the number of the process on it. When the yellow lamp (called an *andon*) goes on, the group leader who notices it goes over to help. After eliminating the abnormality, he or she pulls the switch to turn the light off. But if operations continue without the abnormality being solved, the line stops at a specified position and the red lamp in the andon lights up to indicate the process responsible for stopping the line.

The Toyota production system has a thorough kanban system in its cooperating suppliers' factories, and it is as essential to instill trust in the cooperating companies as it is among the regular Toyota employees. Toyota conducts no inspections of parts supplied by cooperating companies, trusting that there will be no defects. But if there is some defect, the red lamp goes on and the entire production flow stops. Mutual trust between management and employees, between supervisors and workers, or between employees could not exist if employees were *forced* to accept the idea of eliminating waste or if management *forced* them to fit like cogs into the Toyota production system. Without these relationships of trust, the Toyota production system could not function effectively.

Moreover, at Toyota there is an optimistic attitude toward human potential. To waste that potential is considered an offense against a person's humanity. In the Toyota production system, having a worker perform a wasteful operation is seen as wasting a person's skill. When time is spent just waiting, for instance, a person's skills should be utilized for other operations. This notion gave birth to the idea of multifunction processing. When Ohno introduced this revolutionary change, there was a lot of resistance to it, especially among the veteran workers. The conventional way of doing things had been to have one worker for one machine, but now one worker would be operating several machines.

Ohno was not in a position of high authority when he first took up the challenges involved in the Toyota production system. In the case of the veteran workers, especially, he was taking the jobs they had been proud of doing for so long and turning them into jobs anyone could do. It was tantamount to rejecting the way things had been done so far. The veteran workers may even have felt that they themselves were being rejected.

The Toyota production system that Ohno had tried so hard to popularize gradually expanded throughout the company, in spite of all the criticism directed against management and Ohno from superiors, colleagues, and subordinates who resisted what was being done. In the long run, these people gradually came to have more and more trust in him. This, along with management's confidence in Ohno enabled him to complete his work on the Toyota production system.

The growth of people's trust in Ohno can perhaps best be understood in light of the fact that the most important component of the Toyota production system is the trust that is placed in people.

Toyota: A Group of Individualists

Ohno's style was one of "rugged individualism." If Toyota were a place that smothered individualism, then a personality like Ohno's would not have been tolerated.

In some companies when an employee of outstanding individualism distinguishes him- or herself, and uses methods different from previous customs, it is said to be an unsuitable way to do things at the workplace, and great efforts are made to nip this kind of behavior in the bud. Companies where this is done certainly suppress individualism – and because individuality is suppressed, its appearance is conspicuous.

Perhaps individualism like Ohno's could continue to exist because various other individualities also existed in at Toyota. Toyota is not a group that suppresses individuality. Ohno's individualism was accepted precisely because it is a group that overflows with individuality. At many companies, for instance, it is hard to continue working while being a Communist Party member, but at Toyota, Communist City Council members are accepted. Companies with consolidated management of employees, where employees are treated like cogs in a machine, are unlikely to recognize this kind of individualism. In 1977, Representative Michiko Tanaka, of the Japan Communist Party, took up the issue of the "harm" done by the Toyota production system.

Representative Tanaka felt that Toyota took advantage of its dominant bargaining position and forced its management techniques on cooperating companies to turn them into cogs of the Toyota production system. In her opinion, although Toyota made unprecedented profits, the subcontractors took all the risk.

As Representative Tanaka put it:

> *In Toyota's thoroughly rationalized production system, sub-contracting companies are given strict instructions to store specified parts both currently and in the future. Toyota, therefore, does not have to stock extra parts nor finance warehouses. However, if goods are not delivered exactly as specified, contracts are canceled and Toyota ruthlessly proceeds to deal with a third, fourth, or fifth subcontractor. Production estimates have to be made, and when these go awry, the subcontractors incur all losses involved.*

Subcontractors, Tanaka felt, have no choice but to put up with these harsh demands if they want Toyota's business.

A public fact-finding committee announced its opinion in 1978 about the Toyota production system, which Representative Tanaka treated in the Diet without sufficient understanding. The committee's opinion was that transactions based on the kanban supply system between Toyota and cooperating factories were not in conflict with subcontracting law.

The fact that Toyota states its goal as to hold differences in supply amount between unofficial production plan announcements and the kanban orders to less than 10 percent is recognition that differences in amounts do in fact exist. Toyota, however, makes these unofficial plan announcements three months in advance and later adjusts the plans in an effort to make them very accurate so that supply amount differences will be small. Moreover, the economic efficiency resulting from introducing the kanban supply system among cooperating factories completely absorbs these small differences.

Ohno, the father of the Toyota production system, said the following about conditions at the time when the kanban system was introduced into the cooperating factories:

> *It was only in 1962 that we could manage the kanban system company-wide. After achieving this, we called the cooperating firms and asked them to study it by watching how it really worked. These people knew nothing about kanban and making them understand it without a textbook was difficult.*
>
> *We asked the cooperating firms from nearby to come, a few at a time, to study the system. For example, the outside die press people came to see our die press operation and the machine shop people came to see our machine shop. This way of teaching gave us the ability to demonstrate an efficient production method in an actual production plant. As a matter of*

fact, they would have had difficulty understanding the system without seeing it in action.

This teaching effort started with the cooperating firms nearby and spread to the Nagoya district. In the outlying Kanto district [the Tokyo area], however, progress was delayed in part due to the distance. However, a bigger reason was because part makers in the Kanto district were supplying their products not only to Toyota but to other companies as well. They felt they could not use the kanban system just with Toyota.

We decided that this would take time for them to understand, and we set out patiently. In the beginning, the cooperating firms saw kanban as troublesome. Of course, no top managers of production departments showed up in the beginning. Usually people in charge of the operation would come, but no one very important.

*At first, I believe, many firms came without knowing what was involved. But we wanted them to understand kanban and if they didn't, Toyota employees would go and help. People from nearby firms understood the system early although they faced resistance in their companies. And today it is a pleasure to see all this effort bear fruit.**

It is completely off the mark to say that Toyota took advantage of a superior bargaining position to force cooperating companies to introduce the kanban system. Rather, it is quite clear that Toyota sought to cooperate with those factories that could not understand the kanban concept and kept investing time and steady efforts on their behalf until they understood.

The reactions of cooperating factories seem to have been exactly the same as those of Toyota's own production sites

---

* Ohno, op. cit., at 34-35.

when Ohno tried to nurture and establish the Toyota production system. But in spite of the initial resistance, the cooperating factories eventually came to understand that this system was based on trust among people and that it involved a high degree of economic efficiency.

The Relationship of Mutual Trust between Labor and Management

In 1962 the Toyota Labor-Management Declaration was signed by both management and the union. In this declaration, "mutual trust between management and labor" was loudly proclaimed:

> *Mutual understanding between union and management has been built up after passing through various vicissitudes. While management recognizes that people are the source of the company's prosperity and will strive to maintain and improve labor conditions, the union recognizes the need to improve productivity and will cooperate vigorously with all company policies for the sake of the company's prosperity.*

The following four items were written down as concrete measures that labor and management would try to implement by cooperating with each other:

- Improving the quality and performance of products.
- Reducing costs.
- Establishing a mass production system.
- Improving labor conditions and employment stability as a result of these measures.

This declaration of management and labor did not receive quick and unanimous approval; it was a long time in the making. Both management and union had to undergo a number of ordeals before this declaration came into effect.

The worst of those ordeals took place in 1949 and 1950. Management had been weakened by the 1949 recession in the wake of the Dodge Line economic reform policies, and in the following year, 1950, Toyota faced a bankruptcy crisis. Although the Japanese economy was gradually beginning to recover after World War II, disruptions, including the Dodge recession, were still dragging on.

For the first time since the war, Toyota was developing a small-size automobile, the SB sedan, but the cars did not sell well in the economic environment of that time. Furthermore, most car sales needed some kind of financing, so cars were either sold at discount for cash or sold for promissory notes to customers without established credit. Selling at a loss was unavoidable in this situation. Unplanned selling resulted in unplanned production. This was the main reason why management deteriorated.

In the summer of 1949, Toyota entered its worst period. Unless it could raise ¥200 million ($1.5 million), bankruptcy would result. Trucks were the main products at that time and companies accounted for more than half of the customers who bought them. But Toyota's safes contained only promissory notes from those customers. In this kind of situation, requests to commercial banks for financing would most likely have been turned down. Since nothing else could be done, help was requested from the Nagoya branch of the Bank of Japan.

After careful study the Nagoya branch of the Bank of Japan decided that a Toyota bankruptcy would have a major effect on the economy of central Japan. The Bank of Japan then mediated with various commercial banks to get financing for Toyota. Bank financing conditions were as follows:

- The sales company was to be made independent and separate from Toyota Motor Company.

- Toyota Motor Company was to produce only the number of vehicles that could be sold by the sales company.
- Appropriate measures were to be taken to deal with excess personnel.

In addition to these conditions, moreover, the banks held Kiichirō Toyoda, then company president, responsible for Toyota's financial crisis. Consequently, Kiichirō was removed from the position of president and Taizo Ishida, former clerk for Sakichi Toyoda, became the new president. Shotaro Kamiya, having been continuously in charge of sales at Toyota Motor Company, became the first president of Toyota Automobile Sales right after it became separate and independent. Toyota Motor Company and Toyota Automobile Sales continued as a "double feature system" until they were combined on July 1, 1982.

In regard to the first two bank financing conditions, the new management system began with the separation of Toyota Motor Company and Toyota Automobile Sales, but there was a problem with the third condition. Toyota had signed a Labor Cooperation Agreement in 1946, a time when the storms of labor disputes were raging all over Japan. In that agreement, Toyota promised that "employees shall not be fired, no matter what the reason." If the third condition were implemented, it would be a violation of this agreement. If it were not implemented, the bank would not provide financing, and bankruptcy would be inevitable.

After agonizing over this situation, management presented the union with a statement on April 22, 1950, announcing a Reconstruction Plan whose main points included production cutbacks and a 10 percent wage cut. Monthly production of trucks, the company's main product, was reduced from 1,500 to 850, and the 1,600 employees no longer needed because of this move were to be fired.

The union, of course, opposed this reconstruction, citing the 1946 Labor Cooperation Agreement, and made its steadfast resistance clear by calling a strike. The dispute developed into a court case when the union appealed to the district court for a provisional injunction to prohibit the firing. The Nagoya district court, however, recognized the company's claim that the Labor Cooperation Agreement was invalid.

The company survived these firings and for the first time accepted the fact that labor union activities were an integral part of the company. Management presented its reconstruction proposal to the union in an emergency situation when it could not receive financing from the bank unless it fired those workers who were not needed, at a time when the very survival of the company was at stake. The most important thing was to stabilize the management foundation to prevent this unfortunate situation from ever occurring again. These were the reasons behind management's Reconstruction Plan, a public announcement promising to make every effort possible.

The union side also undoubtedly realized some of the implications of the Reconstruction Plan. Although the district court had ruled the Labor Cooperation Agreement invalid, the dispute was ended suddenly and completely. Both labor and management tried to put themselves in each others' places.

In 1960, 10 years after this dispute, import restrictions were lifted and capital was liberalized. At the same time, Japanese manufacturers had to compete with foreign manufacturers who were sending low-priced high-quality cars into the Japanese market. The only way to deal with this situation was to implement quality control and cost reductions so that the company could make cars that were cheaper and better

The signing of the 1950 labor-management memorandum at the end of the labor dispute over Toyota's reconstruction.

than the foreign cars. Understanding that cooperation was essential for this, Toyota management and the union drew up the Labor-Management Declaration in 1962. The seeds of mutual trust between labor and management, which had been so hard to plant during the postwar years, had now grown and blossomed.

It has been stated time and again that the Toyota production system is a production method for producing cheaply a wide variety of items in small quantities. The cooperation of the labor union at Toyota was essential for getting this system to function smoothly. 1962, the year of the Toyota Labor-Management Declaration, was also the year when the Toyota production system was introduced throughout the whole company.

Ordinarily, the relationship between rationalization policies and labor unions is expected to be characterized by in-
compatibility. Cost reduction is rationalization for
eliminating waste, and the Toyota labor union had declared
that it would work together with management to achieve
such rationalization. It could be said that this agreement con-
tradicted the reason for a labor union to exist. Both labor and
management at Toyota had, however, suffered a great deal
before reaching this sort of management-labor relationship.
For both labor and management, the result of enduring the
"great sacrifice" of 1950 was a common perception that stability in management is indeed the only way that management and labor can survive.

Labor-management cooperation was not forced on labor in
a one-sided manner by management. Nor, of course, was the
Labor-Management Declaration forced on labor. The declaration was worked out by the union, based on past experiences
for which it had paid a great price. If management had not
recognized that labor and management were equals, the joint
declaration probably would not have been possible.

Generally speaking, in "company" labor unions, the activities policy indicated by management is automatically approved by pro forma procedures. In the elections of
leadership also, the candidates recommended by management are again automatically approved. It is unthinkable to
have opposing candidates who are selected on the basis of
an election.

In the Toyota labor union, however, there are always opposition candidates other than those recommended by management, and elections to settle the matter. The candidates go
around to the workplaces, express their views, and appeal for

support. If the Toyota union were controlled by management, this would almost certainly not happen.

Evidence of a Group of Individualists

People at Toyota come together from many places. In a world where people are so mobile, and all kinds of information are readily available to everyone, a uniformity of values cannot be expected.

Eiji Toyoda once said, "Regardless of whether a person is young and inexperienced, no matter what kind of person someone is, he or she will become an excellent Toyota person three months after entering the company." These remarks do not imply forcibly converting people. There is no doubt that what Eiji Toyoda meant was that the employees and the environment reinforce each other with an independent spirit.

The more Toyota is praised for its power in accepting the challenge to eliminate waste throughout the company, the more it gets a reputation as a company that suppresses the individuality of its employees so that they all look the same – a group whose members are tightly controlled by the administration.

It is clear, however, that a system like the Toyota production system would not be able to function in such an environment. In fact, the Toyota production system could only be introduced in a group that accepted the challenges of independence and individuality. A free atmosphere conducive to the individuality and independence of employees is really the Toyota company climate.

The Creative Idea Suggestion System is proof of this fact. In this system individuals or small groups such as QC circles make improvements with their creative ideas in five key areas:

1. Improvement in work methods, machines, tools.
2. Economizing in materials and consumables.

3. Improving administrative skills; establishing a management system.
4. Improving the work environment; preventing accident damage.
5. Improving automobile performance; improving precision of manufactured goods.

As is clear from looking at these five areas, creative ideas are implemented to make the original work more efficient. The Creative Idea Suggestion System is work, therefore, that is strictly outside the scope of one's own regular work.

During working hours, filling out suggestion forms and so on is not permitted. Employees use rest breaks or the time at the company after finishing work or the time after returning home for thinking of improvement suggestions and writing them down on suggestion forms. They receive no overtime pay for these activities, and remuneration in the form of awards is only for suggestions that have been adopted. The amount of award money for an excellent suggestion is not insignificant, but there are not that many excellent suggestions submitted. The money received, moreover, is hardly ever used for the enjoyment of the individual, but rather for friends at the workplace.

In spite of this, the number of suggestions submitted in a year come to as many as two million. Who could ask for more convincing proof that employees are actively involved in the Creative Idea Suggestion System?

The Creative Idea Suggestion System that began in 1951 did not emphasize quality in suggestion content, but rather attached importance to maintaining quantity. And this was indeed because of the importance attached to the independence of employees involved in this system. If the Toyota Creative Idea Suggestion System had been forced on people from above, this system could not have blossomed into what it is now.

There is also a pursuit of quality in suggestions. Quality is sought especially from employees who are already submitting excellent suggestions. A person's problem consciousness, focused on work improvement, must be raised higher to improve the quality of suggestion content. If one tried to force employees to improve quality, they would probably respond by just going through the motions; being forced to accept the challenges of work improvement will not raise problem consciousness at all. Problem consciousness begins to emerge only when employees are independently motivated to cope with the situation.

There are many different levels among those employees involved in the Creative Idea Suggestion System, and quality is especially sought from people who have some experience writing suggestions. For people who have only limited experience with the suggestion system, priority is given to maintaining quantity, so that they may first learn to cope independently in this.

The on-site check is a useful means for ensuring quantity. With this method, the idea, whatever it might be, is put into practice at the workplace. If it is feasible, it is submitted as a suggestion. When a proposal that is actually tried out runs into difficulties, the contents of the suggestion are further examined by the person who submitted it.

Because only those suggestions that have been demonstrated to be feasible can be submitted, the adoption rate is high. Adoption builds confidence, and the person who makes a suggestion then becomes independently motivated and involved in the Creative Idea Suggestion System. Because suggestions are tested and refined as necessary, no one ever has to be told, "Your suggestion is no good," which would have a devastating effect on the spirit of the person who submitted the suggestion and cause him or her to shy away from any more participation.

Power from a Respect for Independence and Individuality

Not all Toyota employees participate in the Creative Idea Suggestion System. There are many levels of employees, and some refuse to participate in it.

There was a certain Toyota employee who refused to submit suggestions with the excuse that "I'm not good at expressing myself in writing." His supervisor at the workplace urged this employee to submit suggestions anyway. But because putting suggestions in writing was so hard for the employee, he stubbornly kept on refusing. So one day his supervisor said, "Well then, if you can't write so well, how about dictating it to me, and I'll write it down?" The employee grudgingly responded to the urging of his boss.

Several days later, the employee came to the supervisor to talk about the contents of a suggestion he had thought of. The content was such that it could not possibly be adopted. So the boss modified what he had heard, entered it on a suggestion form, and submitted it. The suggestion was adopted, and an award of ¥500 was received (the smallest award).

It is no exaggeration to say that the suggestion was the boss's. The boss, however, told the employee that his suggestion had been adopted, and handed over the ¥500 to him. On receiving it, the employee smiled broadly and bowed.

This employee then submitted one suggestion after another. When we look at his case, it is clear that until he became involved he considered the Creative Idea Suggestion System to be irrelevant to a person like himself. Although he had the help of his boss, he was actually able to acquire an award of ¥500. It is no doubt true that for this employee, his greatest thrill, more than receiving an award, was his involvement in the suggestion system that he had firmly believed was not for him. After his first success, this employee would return home after work, think about the contents of suggestions with the help of his wife, and then write them down on suggestion forms, submitting one suggestion after another.

The ease or difficulty of submitting suggestions varies according to the workplace, with some places making it easy to submit suggestions and other places making it difficult. In another story, an employee near retirement age was transferred from a workplace where submitting suggestions had been difficult to a workplace where it was easy.

In the previous workplace, discouraged by an environment that made it difficult to submit suggestions, this employee had not submitted any suggestions. At the new workplace also, the employee made no effort to submit suggestions, despite the repeated urging of his boss. The new workplace had many young employees. Among them were some who devoted themselves wholeheartedly to suggestion activities and other employees whose suggestions just did not occur to them as they thought they would.

One of these young employees went to that senior employee to discuss the content of a suggestion the younger man was currently working on. At first, the older employee would have nothing to do with him, considering the whole thing ridiculous. But, in the excessive zeal of the young employee there was an attitude of seriousness, and before anyone knew it, both of them were thinking together about how they could make this suggestion a good one.

The boss saw what was going on, spoke to the senior employee the next day, and tried to encourage him again: "Young people are trying as hard as they can, so why don't you also try to come up with a suggestion before you retire?" The senior employee must have wondered what a suggestion was, after avoiding the subject for so long. Stimulated by the younger employee, however, he began to get interested in suggestion activities.

One day, with retirement just a few months away, this veteran employee handed a suggestion form to his boss. It was the only suggestion this employee ever made. He received a ¥500 award and retired from Toyota.

The Creative Idea Suggestion System has unmistakably become a driving force behind Toyota's power. This is also true of the Toyota production system. But these powerful driving forces emerged precisely because they were integrated into Toyota's climate of freedom, where so much importance is attached to the independence and individuality of its employees.

Taiichi Ohno, the father of the Toyota production system, warned that efficiency would not increase if the Toyota production system was followed halfheartedly. As the saying goes, "A little knowledge is a dangerous thing." He emphasized that success comes not from the system itself, but rather from the spirit that supports the system. In other words, there must be a solid enterprising climate, highly valuing independence and individuality. Without these values, there will be no results no matter how excellent a system is introduced.

The same thing is true of the Creative Idea Suggestion System. The driving force behind Toyota's "inexhaustible power" comes from an enterprising climate that attaches great importance to the independence and individuality of its employees.

A Postscript
The Toyota Summary

On October 30, 1935, the sixth anniversary of Sakichi Toyoda's death, a Toyota Summary was put together, based on Sakichi's final instructions. This summary, the contents of which had been company policy for Toyota Motor Company since its establishment, became company policy for all enterprises affiliated with Toyota. The main points of Toyotaism in the 1935 document were:

- With harmony between supervisors and workers, with sincere devotion to work, strive to help your industry and your country reap the fruits of progress.
- By studying and developing your creativity, always anticipate the trends of the times.
- Be on your guard against showy luxury, while making efforts to be more frugal and courageous.
- While maintaining a warm and friendly attitude, improve the atmosphere in your own home.
- Have respect for the gods and the Buddhas, always repay a kindness, and show gratitude.

This Toyota Summary is the spiritual foundation for the entire company. In 1989 it was revised as follows:

- Always think of the customer first, considering the basics of manufacturing, always making products that are outstanding for their high quality, low cost, and technical excellence.
- With a foundation of mutual trust between labor and management, cheerfully make progress as a company highly valuing creativity.
- Stimulate Toyota activities everywhere, inside and outside the company, while cooperating to expand business.
- Contribute to expanding our economy and building up a better living environment for our society by doing business actively all over the world.
- Strive to improve yourself through self-enlightenment, constantly on the alert for any new social or market trends.

The idea of "highly valuing creativity" unmistakably had its roots in the Toyota Summary. The president of Toyota Motor Company, Shoichiro Toyoda, said the following about the recent Summary revisions in a talk he gave at the beginning of the year:

We must keep trying to implement the basic policy ideas (i.e., the Toyota Summary) as we have so far, for they are the source of Toyota's strength. But at the same time, we would like to make them easier for all of you, our employees, to understand in relation to social consciousness or value judgment changes that have accompanied other changes during our times. We have decided on these changes after considering how the contents can be most conducive to gaining the support of persons both inside and outside the company.

The Toyota Creative Idea Suggestion System, which was introduced in 1951, has maintained a balance between the quality and quantity of its suggestions.

It put down strong roots within the company and has endured because Toyota's enterprising climate values creativity highly.

Appendix 1

A Chronology of the Toyota Creative Idea Suggestion System

May 1951	Creative Idea Suggestion System Committee begins (committee chairman: Shoichi Saito, managing director of the company)
June 1952	First Creative Idea Suggestions solicited
February	First outside factory field trip for employees making outstanding suggestions
July	First call for problem suggestions (8 subcommittees decide topics)
December	Individual annual award system begins
Feb. 1953	Company slogan contest initiated ("good products require good thinking" adopted in March)
April	More Creative Idea Suggestion boxes installed
June	Creative Idea Suggestion System second anniversary celebration (informal discussion between people making creative idea suggestion and secretariat, second annual special issue)

June 1955	First call to all employees for special company-wide topic (topic: ashtrays)
July	First example exhibition (suggestions evaluated at ¥1000 ($7.50) or more: Dec. 1954 – May 1955)
June 1956	Creative Idea Suggestion System's fifth anniversary celebration (pamphlet/poster display)
July 1958	First "All-Toyota Creative Idea Suggestion Informal Discussion" (name changed in 1964 to "All-Toyota Suggestion System Study Group")
April 1960	First prefectural office science and technology prize (3 employees received awards for creative ideas related to work)
October	First quality control month special solicitation
June 1961	Celebration of Creative Idea Suggestion System's tenth anniversary (contests for papers, calligraphy, posters, slogans)
June 1964	Distributing Creative Idea Suggestion System guides to all employees
June 1965	Adopting the joint suggestion system
May 1967	Soliciting and establishing Creative Idea symbols
January 1972	Workplace annual award system begins (number of suggestions per person, award given to each division for each cash award winner)

November	Individual yearly award system changes (gold, silver, bronze established; special awards discontinued; awards standardized)
May 1974	Total number of suggestions reaches more than 1,000,000
June 1981	Beginning of Toyota Good Idea (GI) Club for award recipients
June	Total number of suggestions reaches more than 5,000,000 Creative Idea Suggestion System's thirtieth anniversary (celebration improvement example exhibition, slogan contest, distribution of creative idea suggestion handbooks to all employees with technical expertise, and to employees at or above the ranks of subsection manager and foreman)
Dec. 1982	Suggestion quotas discontinued throughout the company
June 1983	Restoration of Toyota Group Creative Idea Suggestion System secretariat exchange group (previously All-Toyota Creative Idea Informal Discussion Group, All-Toyota Suggestion System Study Group)
January 1984	Distribution of *Creative Idea Suggestion Handbook* for office use; the number of suggestions reaches more than 10,000,000
January 1985	Creative Idea evaluation standards revised and unified

January 1986	Revision of creative idea award standards (workplace awards and individual awards included as part of the bronze prize awards)
November	Using optical character recognition equipment to computerize handling of Creative Idea Suggestion System administrative work
1988	The cumulative number of suggestions reaches 20,000,000
1991	Fortieth anniversary of the Toyota Creative Idea Suggestion System

Appendix 2

An Example of the Toyota Creative Idea Suggestion Form

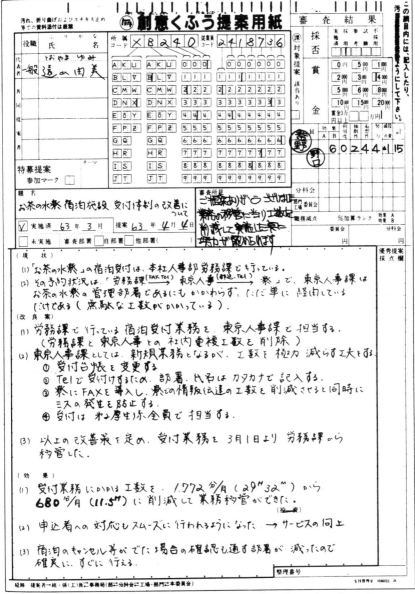

Note: This example was condensed in Figure 1-6 to show the main points of content and scoring. Its topic is described in detail in Chapter 4, Example 1. — Ed.

About the Author

Yuzo Yasuda was born in Chiba-shi, Japan in 1952. As a newspaper and magazine reporter, he covered many facets of the industrial world, including autos, chemicals, steel, banking, and securities. After serving as chief editor of an economic journal, he became a freelance journalist specializing in economic issues.

He is a frequent contributor to *Shukan Bunshun* and *The Tokyo Times*.

Other Books on
Employee Involvement

Productivity Press publishes and distributes materials on continuous improvement in productivity, quality, customer service, and the creative involvement of all employees. Many of our products are direct source materials from Japan that have been translated into English for the first time and are available exclusively from Productivity. Supplemental products and services include newsletters, conferences, seminars, in-house training and consulting, audio-visual training programs, and industrial study missions. Call 1-800-274-9911 for our free book catalog.

CEDAC
A Tool for Continuous Systematic Improvement
by Ryuji Fukuda

CEDAC, or Cause and Effect Diagram with the Addition of Cards, is a modification of the "fishbone diagram," one of the standard QC tools. One of the most powerful, yet simple problem-solving methods to come out of Japan (Fukuda won a Deming Prize for developing it), CEDAC actually encompasses a whole cluster of tools for continuous systematic improvement. They include window analysis (for identifying problems), the CEDAC diagram (for analyzing problems and developing standards), and window development (for ensuring adherence to standards). Here is Fukuda's manual for the in-house support of improvement activities using CEDAC. It provides step by step directions for setting up and using CEDAC. With a text that's concise, clear, and to the point, nearly 50 illustrations and sample forms suitable for transparencies, and a removable CEDAC wall chart, the manual is an ideal training aid.
ISBN 0-915299-26-7 / 142 pages / $49.95 / Order code CEDAC-BK

Productivity Press, Inc., Dept. BK, P.O. Box 3007, Cambridge, MA 02140 1-800-274-9911

Managerial Engineering
Techniques for Improving Quality and Productivity in the Workplace (rev.)
by Ryuji Fukuda

A proven path to managerial success, based on reliable methods developed by one of Japan's leading productivity experts and winner of the coveted Deming Prize for quality. Dr. W. Edwards Deming, world-famous consultant on quality, says that the book "provides an excellent and clear description of the devotion and methods of Japanese management to continual improvement of quality." (CEDAC training programs also available.)
ISBN 0-915299-09-7 / 208 pages / $39.95 / Order code ME-BK

The Service Industry Idea Book
Employee Involvement in Retail and Office Improvement
Japan Human Relations Association (ed.)

This book presents an improvement proposal system in a context designed for customer service and administrative employees. Initial chapters about why suggestions are important and how to write persuasive improvement proposals are followed by two chapters of illustrated examples and case histories from various services industries and office or administrative situations. This is a creative book that should stimulate many ideas of your own. It is a companion to our best selling *The Idea Book: Improvement through TEI*.
ISBN 0-915299-65-8 / 272 pages / $49.95 / Order code SIDEA-BK

Canon Production System
Creative Involvement of the Total Workforce
compiled by the Japan Management Association

A fantastic success story! Canon set a goal to increase productivity by three percent per month — and achieved it! The first book-length case study to show how to combine the most effective Japanese management principles and quality improvement techniques into one overall strategy that improves every area of the company on a continual basis. Shows how the major QC tools are applied in a matrix management model.
ISBN 0-915299-06-2 / 251 pages / $36.95 / Order code CAN-BK

The Best of TEI
Current Perspectives on Total Employee Involvement
Karen Jones (ed.)

An outstanding compilation of the 29 best presentations from the first three International Total Employee Involvement (TEI) conferences sponsored by Productivity. You'll find sections on management strategy, case studies, training and retraining, kaizen (continuous improvement), and high quality teamwork. Here's the cutting edge in implemented EI strategies — doubly valuable to you because it comprises both theory and practice. It's also amply illustrated with presentation charts. Whether you're a manager, a team member, or in HR development, you'll find The Best of TEI a rich and stimulating source of information. Comes in handy 3-ring binder.

ISBN 0-915299-63-1 / 502 pages / $175.00 / Order code TEI-BK

20 Keys to Workplace Improvement
by Iwao Kobayashi

This easy-to-read introduction to the "20 keys" system presents an integrated approach to assessing and improving your company's competitive level. The book focuses on systematic improvement through five levels of achievement in such primary areas as industrial housekeeping, small group activities, quick changeover techniques, equipment maintenance, and computerization. A scoring guide is included, along with information to help plan a strategy for your company's world class improvement effort.

ISBN 0-915299-61-5 / 264 pages / $34.95 / Order code 20KEYS-BK

Better Makes Us Best
by John Psarouthakis

A short, engaging, but powerful and highly practical guide to performance improvement for any business or individual. Focusing on incremental progress toward clear goals is the key — you become "better" day by day. It's a realistic, personally fulfilling, action-oriented, and dynamic philosophy that has made Psarouthakis's own company a member of the Fortune 500 in just ten years. Buy a copy for everyone in your work force, and let it work for you.

ISBN 0-915299-56-9 / 112 pages / $16.95 / order code BMUB-BK

Productivity Press, Inc., Dept. BK, P.O. Box 3007, Cambridge, MA 02140 1-800-274-9911

A Study of the Toyota Production System
From an Industrial Engineering Viewpoint (rev.)
by Shigeo Shingo

The "green book" that started it all — the first book in English on JIT, now completely revised and re-translated. Here is Dr. Shingo's classic industrial engineering rationale for the priority of process-based over operational improvements for manufacturing. He explains the basic mechanisms of the Toyota production system in a practical and simple way so that you can apply them in your own plant.

ISBN 0-915299-17-8 / 294 pages / Price $39.95 / Order code STREV-BK

Also from Productivity

TEI Newsletter TEI — Total Employee Involvement — can transform an unproductive, inefficient, even angry work force into a smart, productive, cooperative team. Learn how by reading the monthly TEI Newsletter. Its articles, interviews, suggestions, and case histories will help you promote a learning organization, activate continuous improvement, and encourage creativity in all your employees. To subscribe, or for more information, call 1-800-888-6485. Please state order code "BA" when ordering.

COMPLETE LIST OF TITLES FROM PRODUCTIVITY PRESS

Akao, Yoji (ed.). **Quality Function Deployment: Integrating Customer Requirements into Product Design**
ISBN 0-915299-41-0 / 1990/ 387 pages / $ 75.00 / order code QFD

Asaka, Tetsuichi and Kazuo Ozeki (eds.). **Handbook of Quality Tools: The Japanese Approach**
ISBN 0-915299-45-3 / 1990 / 336 pages / $59.95 / order code HQT

Belohlav, James A. **Championship Management: An Action Model for High Performance**
ISBN 0-915299-76-3 / 1990 / 265 pages / $29.95 / order code CHAMPS

Christopher, William F. **Productivity Measurement Handbook**
ISBN 0-915299-05-4 / 1985 / 680 pages / $137.95 / order code PMH

D'Egidio, Franco. **The Service Era: Leadership in a Global Environment**
ISBN 0-915299-68-2 / 1990 / 194 pages / $29.95 / order code SERA

Ford, Henry. **Today and Tomorrow**
ISBN 0-915299-36-4 / 1988 / 286 pages / $24.95 / order code FORD

Fukuda, Ryuji. **CEDAC: A Tool for Continuous Systematic Improvement**
ISBN 0-915299-26-7 / 1990 / 144 pages / $49.95 / order code CEDAC

Fukuda, Ryuji. **Managerial Engineering: Techniques for Improving Quality and Productivity in the Workplace** (rev.)
ISBN 0-915299-09-7 / 1986 / 208 pages / $39.95 / order code ME

Hatakeyama, Yoshio. **Manager Revolution! A Guide to Survival in Today's Changing Workplace**
ISBN 0-915299-10-0 / 1986 / 208 pages / $24.95 / order code MREV

Hirano, Hiroyuki. **JIT Factory Revolution: A Pictorial Guide to Factory Design of the Future**
ISBN 0-915299-44-5 / 1989 / 227 pages / $49.95 / order code JITFAC

Hirano, Hiroyuki. **JIT Implementation Manual: The Complete Guide to Just-In-Time Manufacturing**
ISBN 0-915299-66-6 / 1990 / 1000+ pages / $3500.00 / order code HIRJIT

Horovitz, Jacques. **Winning Ways: Achieving Zero-Defect Service**
ISBN 0-915299-78-X / 1990 / 165 pages / $24.95 / order code WWAYS

Japan Human Relations Association (ed.). **The Idea Book: Improvement Through TEI (Total Employee Involvement)**
ISBN 0-915299-22-4 / 1988 / 232 pages / $49.95 / order code IDEA

Japan Human Relations Association (ed.). **The Service Industry Idea Book: Employee Involvement in Retail and Office Improvement**
ISBN 0-915299-65-8 / 1990 / 272 pages / $49.95 / order code SIDEA

Japan Management Association (ed.). **Kanban and Just-In-Time at Toyota: Management Begins at the Workplace** (Revised Ed.), Translated by David J. Lu
ISBN 0-915299-48-8 / 1989 / 224 pages / $36.50 / order code KAN

Japan Management Association and Constance E. Dyer. **The Canon Production System: Creative Involvement of the Total Workforce**
ISBN 0-915299-06-2 / 1987 / 251 pages / $36.95 / order code CAN

Jones, Karen (ed.). **The Best of TEI: Current Perspectives on Total Employee Involvement**
ISBN 0-915299-63-1 / 1989 / 502 pages / $175.00 / order code TEI

Productivity Press, Inc., Dept. BK, P.O. Box 3007, Cambridge, MA 02140 1-800-274-9911

Karatsu, Hajime. **Tough Words For American Industry**
ISBN 0-915299-25-9 / 1988 / 178 pages / $24.95 / order code TOUGH

Karatsu, Hajime. **TQC Wisdom of Japan: Managing for Total Quality Control,** Translated by David J. Lu
ISBN 0-915299-18-6 / 1988 / 136 pages / $34.95 / order code WISD

Kobayashi, Iwao. **20 Keys to Workplace Improvement**
ISBN 0-915299-61-5 / 1990 / 264 pages / $34.95 / order code 20KEYS

Lu, David J. **Inside Corporate Japan: The Art of Fumble-Free Management**
ISBN 0-915299-16-X / 1987 / 278 pages / $24.95 / order code ICJ

Merli, Giorgio. **Total Manufacturing Management: Production Organization for the 1990s**
ISBN 0-915299-58-5 / 1990 / 224 pages / $39.95 / order code TMM

Mizuno, Shigeru (ed.). **Management for Quality Improvement: The 7 New QC Tools**
ISBN 0-915299-29-1 / 1988 / 324 pages / $59.95 / order code 7QC

Monden, Yasuhiro and Michiharu Sakurai (eds.). **Japanese Management Accounting: A World Class Approach to Profit Management**
ISBN 0-915299-50-X / 1989 / 568 pages / $59.95 / order code JMACT

Nachi-Fujikoshi (ed.). **Training for TPM: A Manufacturing Success Story**
ISBN 0-915299-34-8 / 1990 / 272 pages / $59.95 / order code CTPM

Nakajima, Seiichi. **Introduction to TPM: Total Productive Maintenance**
ISBN 0-915299-23-2 / 1988 / 149 pages / $39.95 / order code ITPM

Nakajima, Seiichi. **TPM Development Program: Implementing Total Productive Maintenance**
ISBN 0-915299-37-2 / 1989 / 428 pages / $85.00 / order code DTPM

Nikkan Kogyo Shimbun, Ltd./Factory Magazine (ed.). **Poka-yoke: Improving Product Quality by Preventing Defects**
ISBN 0-915299-31-3 / 1989 / 288 pages / $59.95 / order code IPOKA

Ohno, Taiichi. **Toyota Production System: Beyond Large-Scale Production**
ISBN 0-915299-14-3 / 1988 / 162 pages / $39.95 / order code OTPS

Ohno, Taiichi. **Workplace Management**
ISBN 0-915299-19-4 / 1988 / 165 pages / $34.95 / order code WPM

Ohno, Taiichi and Setsuo Mito. **Just-In-Time for Today and Tomorrow**
ISBN 0-915299-20-8 / 1988 / 208 pages / $34.95 / order code OMJIT

Perigord, Michel. **Achieving Total Quality Management: A Program for Action**
ISBN 0-915299-60-7 / 1990 / 384 pages / $39.95 / order code ACHTQM

Psarouthakis, John. **Better Makes Us Best**
ISBN 0-915299-56-9 / 1989 / 112 pages / $16.95 / order code BMUB

Robson, Ross (ed.). **The Quality and Productivity Equation: American Corporate Strategies for the 1990s**
ISBN 0-915299-71-2 / 1990 / 558 pages / $29.95 / order code QPE

Shetty, Y.K and Vernon M. Buehler (eds.). **Competing Through Productivity and Quality**
ISBN 0-915299-43-7 / 1989 / 576 pages / $39.95 / order code COMP

Shingo, Shigeo. **Non-Stock Production: The Shingo System for Continuous Improvement**
ISBN 0-915299-30-5 / 1988 / 480 pages / $75.00 / order code NON

Productivity Press, Inc., Dept. BK, P.O. Box 3007, Cambridge, MA 02140 1-800-274-9911

Shingo, Shigeo. **A Revolution In Manufacturing: The SMED System**,
Translated by Andrew P. Dillon
ISBN 0-915299-03-8 / 1985 / 383 pages / $70.00 / order code SMED

Shingo, Shigeo. **The Sayings of Shigeo Shingo: Key Strategies for Plant Improvement**, Translated by Andrew P. Dillon
ISBN 0-915299-15-1 / 1987 / 208 pages / $39.95 / order code SAY

Shingo, Shigeo. **A Study of the Toyota Production System from an Industrial Engineering Viewpoint** (rev.)
ISBN 0-915299-17-8 / 1989 / 293 pages / $39.95 / order code STREV

Shingo, Shigeo. **Zero Quality Control: Source Inspection and the Poka-yoke System**, Translated by Andrew P. Dillon
ISBN 0-915299-07-0 / 1986 / 328 pages / $70.00 / order code ZQC

Shinohara, Isao (ed.). **New Production System: JIT Crossing Industry Boundaries**
ISBN 0-915299-21-6 / 1988 / 224 pages / $34.95 / order code NPS

Sugiyama, Tomo. **The Improvement Book: Creating the Problem-Free Workplace**
ISBN 0-915299-47-X / 1989 / 236 pages / $49.95 / order code IB

Suzue, Toshio and Akira Kohdate. **Variety Reduction Program (VRP): A Production Strategy for Product Diversification**
ISBN 0-915299-32-1 / 1990 / 164 pages / $59.95 / order code VRP

Tateisi, Kazuma. **The Eternal Venture Spirit: An Executive's Practical Philosophy**
ISBN 0-915299-55-0 / 1989 / 208 pages/ $19.95 / order code EVS

AUDIO-VISUAL PROGRAMS

Japan Management Association. **Total Productive Maintenance: Maximizing Productivity and Quality**
ISBN 0-915299-46-1 / 167 slides / 1989 / $749.00 / order code STPM
ISBN 0-915299-49-6 / 2 videos / 1989 / $749.00 / order code VTPM

Shingo, Shigeo. **The SMED System**, Translated by Andrew P. Dillon
ISBN 0-915299-11-9 / 181 slides / 1986 / $749.00 / order code S5
ISBN 0-915299-27-5 / 2 videos / 1987 / $749.00 / order code V5

Shingo, Shigeo. **The Poka-yoke System**, Translated by Andrew P. Dillon
ISBN 0-915299-13-5 / 235 slides / 1987 / $749.00 / order code S6
ISBN 0-915299-28-3 / 2 videos / 1987 / $749.00 / order code V6

TO ORDER: Write, phone, or fax Productivity Press, Dept. BK, P.O. Box 3007, Cambridge, MA 02140, phone 1-800-274-9911, fax 617-868-3524. Send check or charge to your credit card (American Express, Visa, MasterCard accepted).

U.S. ORDERS: Add $4 shipping for first book, $2 each additional for UPS surface delivery. CT residents add 8% and MA residents 5% sales tax.

INTERNATIONAL ORDERS: Write, phone, or fax for quote and indicate shipping method desired. Pre-payment in U.S. dollars must accompany your order (checks must be drawn on U.S. banks). When quote is returned with payment, your order will be shipped promptly by the method requested.

NOTE: Prices subject to change without notice.